PLURALIST POLITICS AND POEMS ON REVERENCE LOVE AND SORROW

PLURALIST POLITICS AND POEMS ON REVERENCE LOVE AND SORROW

Har Charan Singh "Chan"

KALPAZ PUBLICATIONS
DELHI-110052

Pluralist Politics and Poems on Reverence Love and Sorrow

Rs. 450.00

ISBN: 81-7835-651-1

Published in 2008 in India by
Kalpaz Publications
C-30, Satyawati Nagar,
Delhi-110052
E-mail: kalpaz@hotmail.com
Phone : 9212729499

Laser Typesetting by: Quick Media, Delhi
Printed at : Vishal Kaushik Printers Delhi

Dedication

To my revered demised parents — Sardarni Ishar Kaur wife of Captain Kartar Singh and my demised life companion Smt. G K Saberwal MA MEd who stood by me through all ups and downs of life for 43 years and gave birth and brought up our two intelligent, hard working and honest sons.

Herman Prit Singh IPS now I.G. Police and Simar Prit Singh who at the age of 22 became youngest editor of NIIT Computer Magazine and who is now the chairman and MD of Compare Infobase which employs more than 700 qualified and intelligent young men and women in the field of Information Technology; and to their equally brilliant life companions — Smt. Binwant Kaur, Associate Professor NIFT Kolkata and Smt. Harmeen Kaur, Fashion Designer of M/s Harmeen Designer's Symphony and Director of Compare Infobase.

Contents

Preface

Pluralist Political Philosophy of Laski I am indebted to Indian Council of World Affair, Sapru House where from 1952 to 1960 I spent all the spare time after attending office reading and writing and having discussions and exchange of views with friends and regular visitors like Dr. J D Sethi. Who was lecturer in Camp College in New Delhi at that time and finally with education and dedication became member of Planning Commission of Govt. of India and Shri Jagmohan who had then recently come from Punjab as Asst. Secretary Delhi Development Authority and rose to becomc chairman DDA, then Governor and thereafter a Minister and finally Shri M L Dhawan who was class fellow of Shri Jagmohan in Lahore and served in UPSC in various capacities till his retirement.

Dr. M.S. Venketaramni, Additional Director - School of International Studies, Sapru House, inspired me to continue my study and same research and journalistic writing. My first article on QUEMOY in world politics was published in Sunday Tribune's Magazine section and subsequent articles in Parliamentary Studies and 'Contemporary' magazines. I continued to write Afro-Asian diary for a number of years for a local weekly - Delhi Times. In the meantime continued my studies and research on Professor Harold Laski.

Poems on Reverence Love and Sorrow, Originally I wrote, these poems in Punjabi which were published in 'PAYYAR TE ROSSA'. I have been writing occasionally poems in Punjabi since my college days in 1950-52 and thereafter, about love failure and reconciliation. Some poems I wrote on Man's Conquest of Moon as I was thrilled by this breakthrough in outer space. Some, I wrote on anti-Sikh riots in 1984 as I suffered and saw with my own eyes my house being attacked and glass panes being broken. We were unable to move out for three days. This was the biggest shock after partition riots of 1947. I owe to my dear friend Shri M.L. Dhawan for encouraging me to write more and to translate those Punjabi poems into English.

H.C. Singh

Introduction

In the present crisis facing *preface* Indian Polity, which is perhaps the worst since independence, Laski's political philosophy is relevant on sovereignty and state's place in a pluralistic society. For a multilingual, multicultural multireligious and multiethnic country like India, theory of pluralism, as enunciated by Laski, is central to the State and its honest implementation by Central Government vis-a-vis Constituent Federal Units is a dire necessity. Pluralism implies that the State is sovercign, the rights of its citizens to voluntarily join associations like cultural and religious societies, trade and professional unions have to be recognized and respected.

Laski's political views on democracy, socialism and communism, will remain relevant whether communism survives in modified form, by taking away from State's control of some means of production and distribution as is now being attempted in China and Vietnam or it dies in it's Stalinist dictatorial form as has happened during last 20 years as is evidenced by the disembersement of U.S.S.R. balkanisation of Yugoslavia and civil war between

Azerbaijan and Armenia. Democracy, where will of the people prevails, will continue as a system of good government as in UK, Japan and Canada or, if it is vitiated with corruption, rigging of ballots and bank scams and kickbacks to fill the coffers of politicians and political parties as in India, Pakistan and vast majority of Afro-Asian Countries; whether State as instrument of Coersion withers away as Marx predicted (which never seemed to happen anywhere) or becomes a fascist movement to silence dissent within the country by sending thousands to torture camps in Siberia during Soviet regimes and killing in gas chambers six millions Jews, as German Nazis did during Second World War.

In early 20's of 20th Century as a lecturer in USA Laski had led a strike and was practically thrown out of the New World as a dangerous Red Professor. Thereafter he settled in UK as Professor of Political Science in London School of Economics and remained so for more than 25 years till he passed into history in 1950. In London undaunted by insults heaped in USA, he plunged into politics, joining hands with Fabian Socialists and became a member and ultimately Chairman of British Labour Party. Along with Sydney and Beatrice Webb, George Bernard Shaw and other socialist intellectuals of various hues, he ceaselessly strived, through his teachings in London School of Economics, writings in monumental books like Grammar of Politics, pamphlet and articles, lectures in Labour Party meeting, Miners Union and other forums, to warn British and Western world against the rise of German Nazism, Japanese Fascism and war clouds that were hanging over and threatening unprotected and weak countries like Poland, Czechoslovakia and other small neighbours of Germany in Europe, and Korea and Manchuria in Asia. Laski strived to caution his countrymen and other democracies to restructure, because bloodshed and destruction was inevitable as a consequences of redefinition of class relations through revolutions. His career, as he was no dogmatic socialist, wavered between Democratic Socialism, i.e., slow transformation.

Though on getting disappointed over the rise of Nazism in Germany he embraced communism and proclaimed it so in his book why I am a communist; he never took divorce from humanism and democracy. The conflict in his mind between democracy and socialism continued till his last breath. He continued relentlessly with his efforts till his death. He continued relentlessly with his efforts to evolve a harmonious society blending the best elements of democracy, i.e., liberty and equality with the best in socialism, i.e., right to work, equal opportunity for education and national health service and old age pension for all. His aim was to bring out a synthesis between democracy of UK and France and Socialism. He did not succeed in his lifetime. The sudden demise of Soviet Communism and hurried modification of Chinese Communism has proved that Laski was right in his approach and he had seen light at the end of tunnel which he could not explain in convincing terms to men like Nixon and John Foster Dullas intoxicated with power and capitalistic arrogance. Harold Laski was undoubtedly one of the greatest political philosophers of 20th Century. His students, admirers and friends became leaders, Prime Ministers and Presidents in many newly independent States in Asia and Africa. Through Menon, Jawaharlal Nehru, India's first Prime Minister, became Laski's admirer and even of Laski's brand of Socialism in contrast to Soviet Communism.

As Chairman of British Labour Party when Clement Attlee was British Prime Minister, Laski was instrumental in countering Conservative Party's argument against Indian Independence, particularly that of hardened imperialist Prime Minister Sir Winston Churchill who had said in British House of Commons that he had not become His Majesty's first minister "to preside over liquidation of British Empire". Laski saw to it and even admonished Attlee for going slow on Indian Independence. As a result India attained Independence while retaining links with Commonwealth on midnight of 15th August 1947.

This is a humble tribute to Prof. Laski in his centenary year by one, like millions, who got political awakening through the study of his writings. This, too, is an acknowledgement of India's debt of Harold Laski.

Some poems I had written originally in Punjabi at the age of 18-19 as a College Student. Those were about Love and Reverence. Some poems I wrote when as a witness to 1984 anti-Sikh riots when my house in Janakpuri and Gurdwara opposite were attacked. I was so shocked that none of my family members could move out for four days. It was virtually like 1947 partition riots. Meanwhile I had been writing poems on my life, my reverence for my parents and Guru Nanak Devji and finally I wrote a poem on demolition of Babri Masjid which, too, was shocking.

PART–I : LAKSHI AND HIS PLURALIST POLITICAL PHILOSOPHY

1

LASKI'S LIFE AND ATTAINMENTS

This volume is homage to the noble life and lasting contribution of Professor Harold J. Laski to 20th Political thought.

No attempt has been made merely to abridge or summarize Laski's masterpiece, A Grammar of Politics. The author of this volume has simply endeavoured to examine, analyse and interpret Laski's views, both liberal, and Marxian, on contemporary political thought towards the close of 20th century.

Efforts have been made to be impartial but if the reader finds appreciation outbalancing criticism, he may attribute it to the fact that author is like Kingsley Martin more an admirer of Laski than merciless critic. The impossible task of avoiding bias has been merely brushed aside. Instead I have tried, commensurate with my knowledge and understanding, to follow the golden rule of 'conscious sincerity' – "along which road to truth is discovered than can be found on any other".

Since the publication of Contemporary Political Thought by students of late Professor W.A. Dunning,

Recent Political Thought by F.W. Coker and Principles of Politics by Prof. Catlin in which there are a few references to Laski's political concept (particularly pluralism) there has appeared no comprehensive books dealing with the political thought of more recent times, particularly with Laski's political concepts. Kingsley Martin's biography, Harold Laski is quite valuable and inspiring but it is more a political biography than a political analysis, while Herbert Dean's–Political Ideas of Harold Laski is, comprehensive but unsympathetic, because it appears that Deane was haunted by the fear of Macarthyism and took it unto him to condemn Laski for his Marxism.

This volume has not been divided into various periods of Laski but into his salient concepts. Broadly speaking, there are only two phases of Laski's political thought. Formative pre-Marxist liberal stage upto 1937 and the Marxist Fabian Socialist period from 1937 to 1950. As some elements of Marxism have always been present in all of Laski's works, he may be termed as quasi-Marxist during the earlier period.

More or less coordinated views of Laski are found on Property, Rights, Sovereignty and Equality and Liberty in his Grammar. Thus, chapters on these topics are based mainly on the text of Grammar. Laskis other books, pamphlets articles and other material had to the searched and coordinated before examination and interpretation.

Quite a many of Laski's works are not available either in the Indian Council of World Affairs Library or in the Delhi University Library. For a thorough-going research project a trip to London would have been essential. A visit to London School of Economics and Political Science and a look at Laski's personal library and papers would have been of a great help even for this project. But unfortunately, howsoever the author wished, a second visit to England for this specific purpose did not materialize. Thus, there are limitations within which the work has been completed.

No pleasure will be greater than one derived from the knowledge that I have been, at least, partially successful in interpreting Laski's political thought for Afro-Asian people, whose cause he held dear and served till the last breath.

The author is indebted to many of his teachers and friends for their inspiration and encouragement, particularly to his dear friend *M.L. Dhawan* the testimony of which is this volume. Howsoever immense the benefit that I may have derived from talks with them, in fairness, it must be said that conclusions and final interpretations are my own. Thus, for all the shortcomings, omissions and commissions, and the views expressed in the pages of this volume, the author alone is responsible. Suggestions will, however, be highly appreciated.

Like Socrates, Laski believed that virtue is knowledge though unlike the former he was more comprehensive and specific in what he believed. Like Plato, he wrote volumes. The creation of a society where justice (harmony of impulses) would prevail, though he despised without reservation the despotism of even those who possessed knowledge-philosopher kings. Like Aristotle, he was a practical, though less original, genius but he did not share Aristotle's hatred for common ownership of property (means of production and distribution) though he appreciated Aristotle's faith in the versatility of human nature. Like Papalists he was a pluralist (in the earlier state) though he was no Christian and as such instead of dividing sovereignty between the state and the church he distributed it among the voluntary associations and the state. Like Machiavelli, he was child of his times though he had nothing to do with the 'Fox and Lion' policy that the former advocated in his 'Prince', nor with the immorality that is attached with the expression "Machiavellism". Like Rousseau he championed the sovereignty of the people but he did not condemn science and reason and nor did he echo "back-to-nature". Like Mill (J.S.), he valued the liberty of the individual but unlike him he laid stress on the attainment of approximate economic equality as a pre-requisite of liberty because without equality liberty to him appeared something like defence of democracy against socialism. Like Green (T.H.), he accepted consent as basis of law but, more than Green, Laski reduced the state to a utility good in the interest of its citizens. Like Marx he sought to prove the validity of economic interpretation of history, evils of capitalism and virtues of socialism, Laski undertook to advocate, from the platform of British Labour Party radical reforms that would render resort to revolution unnecessary.

Rousseau wrote in his "Confessions" that his mother gave birth to twins, him and fear; while Laski's mother gave birth to a rebel and a genius. A meteor appeared on the horizon of our planet on 30th June 1893 which continued to shine for 57 years. In March 1950 the world was shocked at the disappearance of that light which had illuminated lamps of reason in all the corners of the world, especially in Asia and Africa.

Harold Laski, born in an orthodox Jewish family, was studious and rebellious right from his birth. As Kingsley Martin, Laski's able biographer says Harold was excessively precocious. As a very small boy he spent most of his time reading books whose modern scientific and liberal outlook was wholly in contradiction with strict Judaic ritual and dogma that dictated the household routine. His two phases of educations, the Jewish and the English, continued side by side, unreconciled throughout his school days. Inevitably, there came a time when Harold said to his father: I am English, not Polish, an agnostic, not a Jew; I can not reconcile Maimonides with Mill, nor Ann Veronica with the Mosaic Law.

At the age of 18, an undergraduate, Harold rebelled against his orthodox parents and Judaism and married a Christian Doctor of Genetics, eight years older to him. Ernest Barker, Laski's tutor at Oxford, went to Manchester to attempt, a reconciliation of Harold with his parents but to no results. His parents shut him in the room and withdrew his cheque book and embarrassed his young bride by removing her marriage ring. Not till Harold developed "fainting fits" and not till the warning of the doctor that Harold's condition would improve if he were allowed normal relations with his wife that his parents gave way.

Laski was fortunate, too. He had the rare opportunity of sitting at the feet of Great Masters like H.A.L. Fishers, Ernest Barker and F.W. Maitland. He made the best of his teachers, learning and discussing and thereafter impressing them immensely. He worked and worked hard. His labours were rewarded with a First Class in History and Biet Essay Prize, although in the beginning he had taken up science and eugenics and shown great promise in that field, too.

While at New College, Oxford, Laski had become a member of the Fabian Society, took active part in debates, played tennis and enjoyed pulling legs of speakers artists and politicians by sharp questions. But Harold, during his academic career, was a strange type of Youngman who was apparently for ever content to sit in an easy chair with a writing pad on his lap, a pile of books on political philosophy by his side and unaltering view in front of him.

After completing his education at Oxford Laski took to teaching with almost unparalled devotion. After about six years teaching experience at McGill University and Harvard University, he joined London School of Economics and at the death of Graham Walles, though only 32, became Professor of Political Science, the position he occupied till his death in March 1950. Laski was a gifted teacher, and ideal teacher and a great teacher who was to the London School of Economics what Plato and Aristotle were to their respective academies in Athens and Lycium and, in recent times, what Jowett was to Balliol College and in India, what Rabindra Nath Tagore was to Shantiniketan.

Though Laski's energy and ardent spirit were spent in diverse directions but as, Justice Felix Frank has said, the main stream of his life was teaching. His central significance was definitely that of a teacher and to that calling he gave all that he had. He had a remarkable encyclopedic memory and "a peculiarly impressive quality of being able to support his arguments by reference to an exact page in a book which he would direct his skeptical listener to take down from his shelves or look up in the library".

Besides being excellent teacher Laski was a great speaker from whose mouth, like that of Gladstone and from whose pen like that of Carlyle, beautiful, witty and catchy phrases gushed out. He could speak extempore for hours with the same ease and brilliance on serious subjects of political philosophy or make an election speech for the Labour Party. He was so popular a speaker that vast crowds jostled for a seat at his lecture.

Laski was a prolific writer. He started writing articles at the age of 17 and at the age of 30 he wrote his masterpiece *A Grammar of Politics* which like Marx's Manifesto, though not as much, made history. It has been compared with Plato's Republic and Aristotle's Politics. It appears incredible that within three months vacations Laski wrote this epoch-making book that, in Laski's own words, "supplies anxious readers with a complete guide to social life". Throughout the history of mankind few men perhaps read so much and wrote so much at Laski's speed. According to Martin: "It really made little difference to him where he was; he needed only a chair, a writing pad, which in later years was supported by a board shaped to fit his easy chair, and uninterrupted time to work. His MS whether he was writing letters, articles or chapters of a book always looked the same. The minute and perfectly formed writing covered page after page without an alteration. At the end of day a bunch of letters was mostly filled up and addressed, an article was written for a weekly paper and another couple of thousand words of the book completed. He seemed never to have second thoughts or even to want to rewrite what he had written; at most he would re-read that he had written the day before, to write the last page – an exercise which he found helped him to keep the continuity of thoughts from one day to the next. After a day's writing was done he might go so far as to take a half hours walk with Frida, would enthrall his daughter with another installment of his never-ending serial Ginger Joe, the little boy who ran away from home and joined a circus; and then if no one called for talk, read at a sitting a couple of books on his subject and to end the day by skimming a novel before early bed time."

As a writer Laski made a mark and at the raw age of 30 became as renowned as Justice Holmes was at the mature age of 80. His 'Grammar' became the recognized text in scores of Universities of the English speaking world (It has been translated into may languages including Hindi). Among other books of Laski that made him popular as well as controversial are, Foundation of Sovereignty, Communism, State in Theory and Practice, Liberty in Modern State, Parliamentary Government in

England, Reflections on the Revolution of Our Times, American Democracy, Faith, Science and Reason. Besides books Laski wrote hundreds of articles and book reviews, introduction to Translations and last but not the least, letters. His letters to Justice Holmes published in two volumes give Laski the fame of one of the greatest letter-writers of all times.

Holmes-Laski letters unfold Laski's heart, his humanitarianism, his affection, his politics, his morals and almost all what he was, in pure unadulterated form. Like the historic Friendship of Marx and Engles was Holmes-Laski friendship. Though Marx and Engles collaborated in their political views and some writings, Holmes and Laski cleared their doubts by exchanging thought - involving letters discussing political, social, economic and legal problems of their times. Till Holmes death Laski continued to write long, delightful letters which were like glucose to aging Holmes. In a letter dated April 9, 1932 Holmes wrote to Laski "Your letters are such a pleasure to me that I tremble to think of their being interrupted" and again on July 10, 1932 "Every letter from you is a book – those from me are merely petitions for another". Laski kept on writing 'joy and sustaining' letters and his venerable friend wrote: "One of the greatest pleasure of my working life is a letter from you." Equally great was Laski's friendship with Felix Frankfurter, (in USA) H.G. Wells, Bernard Shaw and Sydney Webb in the U.K.

The list of his friends and admirers is too long to be reproduced here. Suffice it to say that inspite of the fact that after Laski had started drifting towards Marxism and there was a political parting of the ways between conservative Holmes and Socialist Laski and inspite of the realization by both that the chasm of differences between them was widening with the passage of every day, no cracks appeared in the magnificent edifice of their friendship which love of Holmes, devotion of Laski and superb intelligence of both had brought into existence.

As John Stuarc Mill took time to disentangle himself from the political philosophy of his father, James Mill, so, to a great extent, young Laski remained under the influence of half a century older Holmes, till the latter's death in 1935. The moment the restraining influence of Holme left its grip, Laski, in the era of rise of Fascism in Europe, began to realize the hollowness of democracy under capitalism. By 1937, he accepted the Marxian analysis and argued that there could not be democracy without socialism: he started preaching the inevitability of socialism on the ruins of laissez faire civilization.

Politics began to consume more and more of Laski's precious time. Laski was a product of revolutionary age. The mental climate of the years preceding the First World War has been described by an able commentator:

"Once more the human mind grew restless, unmelted against the accepted standards of the day and searched for an ideal of justice, like many previous generations. The sources of this restlessness were many. Science began to become doubtful about itself and the certainty of scientific facts. Youth rebelled against the self-satisfaction of the bourgeoisie, against cities, money, worship and the flatness of modern life. Social reformers and socialists attacked the social inequalities hidden under legal formalism".

It was against this background that young rebel Laski, reacted. He was fired by the enthusiasm of fighting for a new cause, for justice, for the war that Germany had unleashed on England. But nature was to spare this genius from the fatal bullets of the war that destroyed the flower of youth. Fortunately, especially for political science, Laski was rejected on medical grounds, when he appeared for enlistment into military service. He spent the war years in comparative peace and security of North America, winning friends, influencing people and teaching politics. Although Laski showed keen interest in Politics even during his college days by joining the Fabian Society, it was in United States that he first plunged into politics.

The Boston Transcript, whether Mr. Laski is an instructor or a lecturer upon "American Government or

Soviet Government" Not even that, Laski's dismissal was demanded. Though Laski was not dismissed but this episode shock the foundations of his political convictions. Seeds of Marxism in liberal Laski were sown that germinated in 1930's and bloomed in 1937.

In the summer of following years Laski sailed for London, where with the help of Grahm Wallas, Sidney Webb and Lord Haldane Harold got lectureship in the London School of Economics and political sciences. Laski had gained paradise. He at once became important and famous, both as a speaker and a teacher. He addressed mass rallies for labour party, became member of the labour executive and finally its Chairman during 1945-46, most crucial years in the labour politics, for it was the first time that Labour Party had been returned to power with absolute majority.

Usually the non M.P. section of the National Executive of British political parties supports the executive with rare exceptions (the most notable of which is late Harold Laski). He practically dictated the Labour Party executive, by virtue of his knowledge, intelligence, influence and oratory. There was no match to Laski in the Labour Party, either amongst the M.Ps or non M.Ps.

According the Kingsley Martin, Laski had more courage than wisdom to tell Attlee at his face in the presence of his colleagues that he ought to give up the leadership of the Party in deference to some one with more of the essential gifts. He defended himself by saying that Nature meant Attlee for a second lieutenant, that he lacked to drive and imagination his position demanded, that it was more honest to tell him so to his face than to follow the example of colleagues who were intriguing behind his back.

Laski was aware of the distrust of the leaders for him because of his radical views, extra-ordinary intelligence and dominating personality. Once in a speech he indulged in a self criticism:

"Your Chairman (Laski) today is an example of that dangerous species who, so far as my knowledge goes is in our Movement rarely trusted and never praised – the species whose professional work is criticism and thought. I represent something a little different from the past, British by birth, middle-class by origin, Jewish by inheritance - symbolic of the vital fact that the Labour Party knows no boundaries save these which are defined by faith in its principles and policies.

True that Laski could not achieve in pure academic the status of Plato. Neither he could be a revolutionary - philosopher like Lenin, though by temperament, profession and environments he was unfit to be a Lenin but because of his sharp intellect, outstanding brilliance, encyclopedic memory and incessant work, he could be a Marx of our own times. Had he lived for another 15 years, as expected, for the volume and variety of books he had collected specially for writing history of French Political Thought, he might have produced a work as great and epoch-making as the 'Das Capital'. As Marx without 'Capital' was even recognized a great Philosopher so Laski without a book matching the Capital is great.

Kingsley Martin has rightly summed up Laski's failures that he wasted his time in politics and parties, that he should have confined himself to serious thought and that he was doctrinaire and repetitive.

But to sum all this up what do the attacks amount to? That in the last period of his life he taught constantly against failing health and because of his belief in the urgency of his message spent himself unwisely and wore himself out twenty year too soon in the attempt to persuade us to seek salvation before the city of wrath was consumed."

Harold's influence in colonial countries struggling for independence and suffering under the yoke of dreadful imperialism was great. In Europe and America he was the subject of criticism while in Africa and Asia he was the object of reverence.

In no part of the world did Harold have more influence than India: 'Krishna Menon, the first High Commissioner in London of free India and one of Harold's most devoted friends and admirers, represented literally hundreds of Indians who as students came under Harold's spell in England. They owed far less to meetings that he eloquently addressed than to the personal talk and tuition with a philosopher who took it for granted that Indians were the equals of Europeans and who also reminded them when necessary that they were not necessarily their superiors.'

In the view of Professor Hawkins: "To all who are concerned with the scope and function of political authority the ideas of Harold Joseph Laski are of signal importance. Over the course of his life-time Laski's ideas reflected in many respects the strength and weakness both of these who strive to maintain liberty as the main end of democratic government, and of those who see in equality the fountain-head of democracy which is secured largely through state action. Beginning his public career as an extreme critic of the state, Laski had been for many years prior to his death an outstanding spokeman of collectivism. This vigorous personality was one of the most controversial figures in the academic and political life of the 20th century".

But like Herbert A Deane, Hawkings criticises Laski for his Marxism and calls attention to the several unfortunate results of Laski's failure during the years after he accepted Marxism because he attempted to marry liberalism to Marxism.

On the other hand an eminent scholar, Professor William in 1947 wrote about Laski:

"The Lockean Jeffersonian theory of revolution has been vigorously re-affirmed in our own time by Harold J. Laksi. His political thought had sprung from the rich heritage of the liberal faith and his socialism is but an enlargement of his liberalism, into the economic and social aspects of life. His defence of the democratic socialist movements against the inroads of revolutionary communism. While no yogi he never embraced the creed of the commissar".

Though we do not agree that Laski's socialism was merely an extension of liberalism yet there is no doubt that he never advocated communism of Russian type and never earned praise from Moscow. "Reflections on the Revolution of Our Times", a Marxian interpretation of the October Revolution, which was regarded subversive even by socialists in the West was termed reactionary by the guardians of Marxism sitting in Kremlin. In December 1946, M. Alexanderov wrote in *Pravda* that Laski was one of those Professor in "bourgeois countries" who according to Lenin "sell learning to serve the interest of capital and who are ready to utter most improbable non-sense and unconsciousable stupidities and rubbish against the socialists" adding that Laski was serving reaction and working against the interests of the working class.

A few months later, in a similar way Harold was made target of Pravada's attack. Harold was described "as one of the most active participants in the field of anti-Soviet propaganda who specialize mainly in proving the advantages of bourgeois democracy over Soviet socialist democracy".

Equally severe and merciless was criticism of Laski in USA, the country for which he had 'affection'. He was denounced for his socialism and Marxism and was called a "Red trouble-maker" by Mr. Thomas of New Jersey, in U.S. House of Representatives others called Roosevelt Programme as 'Laski Programme' imposed on New Deal thinkers, and finally on the President, by the London Professor of Economics and his friends. The idol of our squab intellectuals and some of older ones.

But Harold Laski was a Marxian socialist. His socialism had its origin in the moral revolt against social injustice and it was not until the capitalist crisis of 1929 that Marxism began to play a dominant part in his political philosophy. The criticisms both in U.S.A. and U.S.S.R. were undeserved. His touchstone was justice, though he championed the Soviet Revolution to the end, there were few more devastating critics of communist tactics, of trials and purges and use of conspiratorial techniques.

Above all though he was honest, he was not prepared to compromise honesty even for the Labour Party whose cause he championed. He remained honestly and even vehemently critical of Labour Party, but he gave it his loyalty to the end.

2

PLURALISM VS STATE SOVEREIGNTY

Laski as a pluralist is the most forceful and sweeping critic of the theory of absolute sovereignty of state. In his 'A Grammar of Politics' he goes so far as to declare that it would be of "lasting benefit to political science, if the whole concept of sovereignty were surrendered" and more particularly the 'arid' and 'unfruitful' concept of legal sovereignty.

The views of Laski and other pluralists are at variance both in the way they attack the traditional theory of state sovereignty and the position they precisely assign to other associations in the pluralist society. Laski is not at one with everything that Dugnit, Figgis, Barker, Cole, Lindsay or MacIver has to say on this subject. While Dugnit attacked the absolute theory of sovereignty mainly from juristic point of view; Figgis sought to provide autonomous right of churches and communities; Barker was concerned more with economic and professional groups, Laski was anxious to assign a place of honour to trade unions. Just like the advocates of idealism, utilitarianism, liberalism and communism, exponents of pluralism laid different and varied emphasis on certain aspects of their theory. Again, like these "isms", pluralism was not a rigid theory as is often mistaken from Laski's radical views and often forgotten that later on Laski himself had abandoned these views as leading to anarchy of association and jumble of trade unions, competing, quarrelling and fighting among themselves. Caker is, therefore, right in defining pluralism in such words. According to him Pluralism, is a term applied to the somewhat varying doctrines which are alike in their common opposition to the traditional theory of state sovereignty.

We are here to examine chiefly Laski's views on this subject, who, as Coker says, is most sweeping and emphatic of all pluralist in his theoretical attack on monistic conception of state sovereignty. No theory of state is created ex-Nihieio. Laski, who, like Machivelli, was amenable to the influence of his age, was not expected to fly in the high airs of abstract imagination. He never created a Utopia like that of Thomas More. Laski, as an exponent of pluralism, shows the influence of Mill and Green who had already questioned the states claim to omnipotence by assigning to the individual a moral personality whose personal liberties state had a duty to safeguard.

"All pluralist theory" says Coker (Including Laski's theory) "shows the influence on the one hand, of earlier sociological and juristic discussion of the states relations to economic and professional groups and, on the other hand, of broader ethical and philosophical ideas as to the value of variety and freedom in self-expression as J.S. Mill's moral and intellectual individualism and in T.H. Green's idealist doctrine of self-realization".

Besides the influence of utilitarianism of Mill, idealism of Green, Fabianism of Webb, Shaw, Juristic discussion on the relations of social and economic group with the state had significant impact on Laski's political thought.

Before we describe the nature, implications and consequences of attack it is relevant to explain in brief the object of attack. Crushing blows have been dealt to the so called absolutist view of state sovereignty. The most sought for target of disparagement is Hobbes concept of absolute sovereignty (and Austin's view of legal sovereignty). In fact case for pluralism is a straight fight between Hobbes and Laski. Both have their supporters and camp-followers. If Hobbes is prince of absolutism, Laski can be regarded standard-bearer of pluralism's attack on absolutism. The former is the godfather of the traditional theory of state sovereignty while the latter has come to be regarded its grave-digger.

Importance of the term 'Sovereignty' to political science is as great as is of term 'value' to science of political economy. Bodin in 16th century wrote in his famous De republica "is the power to give law to all citizens, generally and singly". He further defined sovereignty (majestas) as the "highest power over citizens and subjects, unrestrained by laws". The expression in Bodin's definition 'unrestrained by law' does not in fact mean what it apparently conveys; for Bodin would also have the sovereign subject to "natural and divine laws" and the "laws of the realm". These are obviously the limits on sovereign power who in other fields might be absolute. Bodin armed the sovereign vis-a-vis the church with absolute powers in civil spheres, because Bodin could not stand the frequency (intensity of religious wars, which was the most salient, though notorious hall mark of the age. His was the call for peace against war. He sought to "vindicate the supremacy of secular order against religious claims".

Hobbes, Rousseau and others, who were also, like Bodin, faced with the problem of disintegrating civilization, though differed with Bodin as much as their respective times differed with that of the former, upheld in their own ways what is known as the traditional or orthodox theory of sovereignty.

Thomas Hobbes in his 'Leviathan' made the unlimited and absolute supremacy of the sovereign as keystone of the structure of his political theory. His sovereign is not even subject to divine and natural laws unless these laws are interpreted in the manner acceptable to him. The sovereignty of Hobbes sovereign was so absolute that he did not even allow the existence of corporations in society whom he regarded with contempt as nothing more than "like worms in the entrails of a natural man".

Similarly, Rousseau, though he assigned the sovereignty to the body politic, regarded it as the "sole judge of what is important" for subjection to the general will. Rousseau also deprived the corporations and associations their legitimate place in the scheme of society because he feared that by doing so he would be creating states within states, the diseases from which the 'Ancient regime' was already suffering.

Legal aspect of sovereignty is chiefly associated with John Austin. Austin's definition of legal sovereignty rests on the location of a determinate superior, not in the habit of obedience to a rival superior, who gives commands but receives none. Austin's theory inspite of its merit of legal clarity is artificial, as Sir Henry Maine condemned, to the point of absurdity because "It is worthless as an explanation of modern state for political purposes. No sovereign, not even the sultan of Turkey or Louis XIV who said "I am the state" a Nepoleon or Ranjit Singh, who in their hey day commanded overwhelming obedience, possessed such an absolute and unlimited power of which Austin speaks. It is not our purpose here to analyse the Austinian theory and point out its absurdities but to examine Laski's attitude towards state sovereignty and the resulting doctrine of pluralism.

After having rejected Austin's theory of Legal sovereignty as historically false, politically absurd, legally unsound and impossible of location in a federal state, Laski refutes Austin's suggestion that in England electorate which exercises its sovereignty through its representatives is sovereign. Here is inconsistency in Austin theory which is amply unmasked by Laski.

"For, in the first place", as Laski points out "the Crown and the House of Lords are not representative of the Commons in any sense to which precision can be attached, and when Austin goes on to argue sovereign electorate may delegate its power either subject to a trust or trusts or "absolutely or unconditionally', he fails to remember the logical meaning of a definition which implies the impossibility of alienation. If the electorate merely created the trust", Laski strikes the death blow to the Austinian theory of legal sovereignty the latter would not be a sovereign body. If it created a sovereign body, in the sense Austin gave that term, it would itself cease to be sovereign".

In this way Austinian theory leads to the concept of popular sovereignty - sovereignty of the whole community. Thomas Jefferson is regarded as the first important exponent of this doctrine which found a place of honor in the republican constitution of America after independence. The meaning and explanation of the term popular sovereignty have remained ambiguous. To Jefferson and Americans it meant that "people is the only source of governmental power". To Rousseau and French Revolutionaries it meant the sovereignty of "the general will". Today, as Laski rightly says that it means that in a community the interests which prevails must be the interest of the mass of men rather than any special portion of the community".

We have already examined Laski's attitude towards the absolutist concept of sovereignty, his condemnation of Austinian theory of legal sovereignty and his treatment of the vague idea of popular sovereignty. If acceptance of Hobbesian view of unlimited sovereignty is a challenge to human conscience, if an attempt to locate sovereignty in a 'determinate human superior' is an impossible adventure; if popular sovereignty is nothing but lip - service to human equality, then what exactly is sovereignty? The quest of an answer to this question leads Laski to an analysis of the nature of sovereignty: what in fact sovereignty is and not what it ought to be, or some philosopher thought it to be. Laski states with the belief that 'unlimited power is nowhere in existence' in other words sovereignty under no circumstances can be absolute 'irresponsible' and inimical to the interests of the vast majority of the people. It also means that nobody has a birthright to rule over others, not even an elected representative has a right to perpetuate his rule, even under the cloak of mandate of the people. A Government is, therefore, duty-bound to submit to the judgment of the electorate. In a modern state it implies the prevalence of periodic general elections to national parliament or congress. According to this (Laski's) notion, sovereignty implies the existence and recognition of a "system of rights" of individuals which help them in the realization of their best selves.

Recognition of right by the state and their realization by the individual and association is one of the purpose of the state of civil society. A state may, in fact, honour or violate these rights and work contrary to the sacred purposes but it will continue to be a state and as such sovereign, so long as it is able to control the coercive authority. Sovereignty of the state is, therefore, different from the purpose of the state.

Sovereignty, abjectively speaking is what Laski says elsewhere "supreme coercive power" in a society, which defines 'the way of life to which both individuals and associations must conform". It is by the possession of the coercive authority which is called sovereignty that a state is distinguished from other associations. The 'heart' of sovereignty is the armed forces of the state. "Those who control the use of armed forces are in fact the masters of sovereignty."

Above definition of sovereignty has much in common with the definition of Bodin and Hobbes in the sense that sovereignty is in the last analysis unlimited coercive authority of the state. Although Laski does not locate this sovereignty in a human superior but he recognises its existence as power that compels obedience to the will of the state. In fact the dispute between Laski, the pluralist, and Hobbes the absolutist is not on what sovereignty is but for what purpose it is used. Here is apparent an inconsistency in Laski. At one place we find Laski saying that sovereignty is nowhere unlimited and cannot be irresponsible but at another place he emphasizes the sovereignty is nothing else than the supreme coercive authority in the state. If sovereignty is the armed might of a state that is used to compel obedience to the will of the state then this sovereignty is nothing else than absolute and unlimited sovereignty of which Hobes spoke. Laski appears to be confusing sovereignty what it is with the aim for which it should be used.

So far our attention has been concentrated on the examination of internal aspects of sovereignty. We agree, in principle, with Bodin, Hobbes and Rousseau that, whereever the sovereignty might rest, it is supreme in the sense that is will brook no disobedience, and, positively speaking, state uses the armed forces, at its command, to elicit obedience if it regards disobedience a challenge to its sovereign authority and is convinced that it will amount to revolt. We agree with Laski that absolute and unqualified sovereignty of the state, in domestic sphere, is "incompatible with the interests of humanity". Allegiance of an individual to the whole humanity is an ideal which is incompatible with state sovereignty.

Today possibility of 3rd world war is there because citizens owe allegiance to their states and not to the world or United Nations.

The interdependence of the modern world is well recognized by Laski. Those countries which in the exercise of their sovereign rights waged wars against their neighboring countries and caused immense suffering to the humanity stand condemned. If ever a proof was needed that a check is necessary on the unlimited power of the state it was provided by the 1st and 2nd world wars which brought death and destruction to millions of innocent men and women. Hiroshima and Nagasaki are grim warnings of the terrible consequences of unfettered state sovereignty. Some sort of effective world Government armed with supreme coercive authority (sovereignty) is therefore "axiomatic in any plan for international well-being". In its, absence demon of war will be the "ultimate orbiter of international relations".

The concept of absolute sovereignty is rightly rejected because its bases is that will of the state is the sole source of law, both Municipal and international. If we accept will of the sovereign state as the only source of law then we are led straight into the avenues of war and international anarchy. The most significant cause of wars has been and is the insistence of state sovereignty and resulting absence of a world organization that can compel the disobedient state to remain within the limits of international law, and punish them for the violation of rules of international law. Because of the imperfection of international law, in recent times, Pakistan, in 1947-48 could invade Kashmir, U.S.A. could intervene in Guatemala, and in 21st century Afghanistan and Iraq and Soviet Union could drawn the Hungarian rebellion in blood. Today possibility of 3rd world war is there because citizens owe allegiance to their states and not to the world or United Nations. On the other hand if the possibility of war is ruled out. Which we hope will soon be, it will be so because the war will mean not victory but extinction of both would-be victor and the would-be vanquished and not because soon people will transfer their allegiance from national state to world organization, although this might be the consequence of outlawing of war. It is thus clear that the "notion of an independent sovereign state is, on the international side, fatal to the well-being of humanity. What is required for the moment is not the 'disappearance' of the state sovereignty leaving the world in anarchy but its transfer to the world Government. That alone can guarantee 'inter-national well-being' and make possible the realization of the best life for whole humanity. Everybody and every state wants peace because the whole world is alive to the horrors of nuclear war. But unfortunately they do not realize that so long as state sovereignty remains, the possibility of war will continue to hang like the sword of damocles over the panic-ridden humanity. We agree in Toto with Laski that the salvation of mankind lies in One World in which there will be "no room for separate sovereignties" and "those functions which influence the life of the great society must be subject to common and concerted decision of men".

The problem that Laski posed was, how an individual in a society should be able to acquire a satisfactory balance of impulses so as to be in a creative sense free: An absolute philosophy that of Bodin, Hobbes, and Austin that made the sovereign or the sovereign state all supreme, issuing orders to the citizens was found by Laski inadequate for the moral purpose. He was convinced that a citizen cannot be in a real sense free in a state where law is command of the sovereign or the Government, or the dictator. Laski knew well that man is a bundle of impulses. He has varied and various interests. Each man differs in his ideas and social instincts from the other as much as he differs in face and bodily structure. But yet man, being gregarious by nature is a social animals. This social instinct of man finds expression in his memberships of various associations like churches, cultural societies, trade union and political parties. These associations exist to fulfill purposes which a group of men have in common. There are, therefore, Laski argues, two types of wills: (1) the will of the individual and (2) the group will. The will of a person as an individual and as a member of some association.

Following the footprints of Greike and Maitland, who had studied at length history of corporations, Laski seeks to prove that these corporations, trade unions, religious, economic, cultural and other professional associations come into existence independent of the state. He picks up the threads of arguments left by them and goes on to explain that state is simply one of the associations. It has no special right to demand allegiance save on the ground of functions it performs. The only difference between state and other associations is that membership of state is compulsory: that we are born as members of the state but not as members of trade union, church etc. Such associations arise spontaneously and individuals become their members of their own free will. As such rules of these voluntary associations have as much validity as the laws of the state. If a state does not recognize the independent personality of these associations and refuses to consider validity of their rules equivalent, though not in law but in fact, to the validity of its rules, such a state according to Laski, is sowing the seeds of revolt. Its basis, then, is not consent of the government but the arbitrary authority of the rulers.

It is not only that such associations are voluntary and arise independently but, it is to be noted, these are considered to perform functions which a state is either unable or unwilling to perform. It is also emphasized by Laski and other pluralists that the functions that some of these associations perform are in no case secondary. These might be unimportant or of little importance for the state but for the members of these associations such functions are more useful and necessary. Consequently these associations often inspire loyalties that are deeper than that the state commands because "loyalty is won from us, it cannot be imposed upon us.

Laski was a firm and ardent believer in diversity of human nature. He makes a fine distinction between 'resemblance and identity', the former he regards the outcome of a well ordered society while the latter he condemns as the proof of tyranny. This explains why Laski had terrific hatred for fascism. He lays emphasis that we are never as human beings wholly included in any relation. About us is always an environment which separates us from others, or, at the best, makes our union with them but a partial one. For our minds, so far as social theory is concerned, are finite minds. We know something, but not all things and what we know we know differently from one another".

Laski's object in explaining in detail the diversity of human nature was to bring to light the purpose of social organization. Its purpose is not, as Mussolini argued, to forge unity at all costs but to give recognition to diversity: not to gain the "herd like unity" of which Hitler wrote in Mein Kampf but to emphasise the desirability of pluralistic society. The authority of the state should grow within the conscience of the governed and not be imposed from above, for a "unity achieved without any contribution may adjust me to the new environment it creates but it will not be a creative adjustment". The difference in living under a pluralistic society, which recognises diversity of human nature and inspires cooperation and loyalty in a fascist society, under which everything is for the state, nothing against the state and nothing outside it, is compared by Laski as "between living in one's own house and living in a prison-cell".

After having set forth clearly the advantages of a pluralistic society and disadvantages of living under fascist tyranny, Laski draws the inference that "structure of social organization must be federal, if it is to be adequate", because "its pattern involves, not myself and the state, my groups and the state, but all these and their inter-relationship".

The meaning of the term 'Society is federal, authority must be federal' is that there should not be concentration of authority in one person or organ. For this purpose, it is essential that there should be, firstly a representative system of Government and secondly, more decentralization, particularly functional.

A system of representation is considered essential in the modern age for any state that has its basis consent of the citizens because it is not possible to govern modern states as vast as China, India, Russiti and U.S.A. on the principles of direct democracy. The problem of representation is to enable mass of men to have some share in the government howsoever indirect, periodic and inadequate it might be. Laski grants sufficient freedom to representatives and warns that too much cannot be expected from them. They will not be delegates in the sense either (a) 'making all their views known before hand or (b) submitting their proposed views on new problem back to their constituents for approval'. Nothing more is conceded to the people than their right to elect their representatives once in 'four or five years and, in the case of national emergency, right to put pressure through their groups. As mere right to vote is not enough so is the existence of representative institutions. A reprehensive system to be just must have educated and politically conscious system and exercise discretion in the selection of their representatives. They should also have rights, leisure and minimum economic well being.

3

PLURALISM AND DECENTRALISM

Decentralization of power is a paramount necessity because absolute power is likely to corrupt absolutely those who wield and in the second place is likely to result in its perpetuation and ultimate destruction of civil liberties of the people and their representative institutions, as well as voluntary associations. Decentralization of authority, in this context, has, as Caker says: "two aspects, outside and within thc formal political government: on the one hand in the collective bargaining over wages and the voluntary arbitration of industrial disputes and on the other, in the increasing part taken by associations of labourers, professional men, farmers, manufacturers, traders and bankers in influencing governmental action". As Hsiao asserts, for the pluralists, in general, decentralization is not administrative but functional because administrative decentralization does not effect the absoluteness of the state sovereignty. It is the right of the trade unions to be concerned in the administration of industry and to be consulted in the determination of wages that pluralists like Laski attach importance to. Although pluralists are inclined towards administrative decentralization yet there seems to be "no inseparable bond between pluralism and administrative decentralization". Laski's pluralism involves the making of decisions out of the interests which will be effected by them, and, in turn their application by those interests. For Laski it means self-Government in industries like mining, textile and steel; it also means existence of consultative bodies or representative of the professions, e.g., surrounding the Ministry of Education with bodies entitled to speak on behalf of parties to the educational process and entitled to be consulted because they are entitled to speak. And, for Laski it also means the abandonment of concept of state sovereignty in the sense which 'equates' government with society.

The principle of social organization in the pluralist society of which Laski speaks, is that an individual is entitled to act in the way his instructed conscience directs him. It is the insistence that coordination should grow from within and not imposed from without. Laski's scheme rightly recognises the necessity of a coordinating authority but, be it noted, not of the same, type as was advocated by Hobbes in Leviathan and even as exists in the modern class states of which we have ample experience.

This 'creative coordination' can only be there if for the whole people conditions of decent life exist.

To prove the validity of this Marxian truth Laski reiterates that a man cannot be his "best self, if he is involved in a perpetucal struggle to satisfy the barest minimum of physial appetites". A society to be pluralist and just, must therefore, recognize all the rights postulated by Laski. Freedom of speech is, as already stated, life blood of the society. Without universal education the educated will not have access to power and inclination to perpetuate themselves in power. If vast property is held in private hands, its owner will control the state in their own interest to the exclusion of propertyless who in all probability will be victimized as the (Third Estate) was before the French Revolution.

This type of pluralist society if realized will be a paradise on earth. Because everybody will be guaranteed right to work and will be provided work and an adequate remuneration. There will be abundant production; because everybody will attain education that is necessary for the realization of best in self. There will be peace and harmony; because there will be freedom of speech and association. It will be a golden age in which science and art will achieve unimaginable heights. In such a society nobody will starve, none will be without shelter and clothing nor anybody unlettered. There will be nor rulers nor ruled. It will be a classless, factionless, creedless cooperative commonwealth.

Laski and his pluralist associates thus dealt strong blows on states claim to absolute monopoly of individuals allegiance and absolute authority over their social behaviour. Laski divides the sovereignty into small pieces and distributes these to the associations in accordance with the allegiance they command and appeal they make upon their members. Laski goes on further than other pluralists when he not only devoids the state of its sovereignty but vests that sovereignty in the individual conscience. In this assertion influence of Mill and Green is clearly visible.

Here is the paradox in Laski's thought. He makes the association morally as sovereign as the state, assigns ultimate sovereignty to the individual but still leaves with state the all important functions of coordinating the relations of other associations inter-se and in relation to their members. The difficulty is that Laski is combining the elements of Mills liberalism, Green's positive freedom, Maitland's personality of corporations and also under the increasing influence of Marx's socialism he is trying to steer clear out of the anarchic implications of his attack on the state sovereignty. In this he has failed because no one can succeed. Laski could not become a Marxian socialist by attacking the state from pluralistic and individualistic angles. Neither was it possible for him to remain an individualistic. Neither was it possible for him to remain an individualist by taking increasing doses of scientific socialism of Marx. He had to become either increasingly a follower of Marx or stick strongly to the individualistic theories of Mill. In Laski's mind Mill and Marx were boxing. He could not accommodate both although he very much wished. As the years passed and political horizon in Europe darkened with the Fascist fires and smoke, Marx began to occupy progressively more prominent place in Laski's mind.

"It is perhaps sufficient for me" Laski announces his conversion to Marxism "to say here that I know recognize (so for at least I am concerned) that the pluralist attitude to the state and law was a stage on the road to an acceptance of the Marxian attitude to them.... To limit its (state's) power as the pluralist sought to limit its power we must destroy the class structure of society, for the state is simply the executive instrument of the class in society which owns the means of production".

The faith in human reason granted, there is bound to be disarmament and consequent emergence of a world government. If the dream of world government is realized. Sovereignty, as supreme coercive authority, will then vest in the world government, the United Nations or its successor and the present day nation states will then be reduced to the status analogous to that of units of a federation. The status of U.S.A., for example, in such a scheme will be somewhat similar to what is of state of New York in the Federal structure of U.S.A. of today. Sovereignty as a supreme coercive authority will remain in reality even if there is world government. We do not think that pluralism has either withered away or will wither away. A pluralistic society is an ideal. It will be achieved only when men become so educated, so cultured and so perfect that they render the use of force unnecessary and there comes into existence, in Marx language, a classless society. Under such a classless society there will be no sovereignty or the coercive authority to compel obedience. But even in a classless society a superior coordinating authority will be required to control communication, movement of food-grains and supply of necessities of life to different areas. Such a society will be, to a great extent, pluralistic. There will be numerous autonomous associations, corporations, trade union, cooperative societies, churches, clubs and sabhas to cater to the social, economic, religious, cultural and political needs of men. In this sense pluralism is an ideal which can be attained only if society advances to such a stage that use of force for eliciting obedience is ruled out. In this sense, again, state sovereignty and pluralistic society are mutually exclusive.

Present day state, inspite of its being democratic and socialistic, is a class state where state sovereignty rests with the governments. Though there are various associations, corporations, trade unions and other associations, these ultimately exist by the will of the state. The state is sovereign and not these associations. The sovereign state can even at the risk of revolt, outlaw any or all these association as Hitler, did in 1939. When he became the 'state', outlawed communistic trade unions and Jewish organizations and religion and a host of other association, and as communists after 1947 in Soviet Union forced out of existence church and Kulaks and as the U.S.A. has practically banned the foundation of groups and associations with communistic aims, under acts for prevention of subservient activities.

Sovereignty (absolute sovereignty), therefore, is a fact and will remain so, so long as men do not become saints. As the society advances and necessity for the use of coercive power decreases there will be more of pluralism. It is not enough to conclude, as Coker does that pluralists expressed the 'prevailing trends' in recent political thought and have been valuable in demonstrating the importance of role played by voluntary associations and groups are 'intermediate' between the individual and the sovereign state. Pluralists and especially Laski were in fact thinking of a just society which they thought must be pluralistic. It was an ideal. Recognition of diversities in human nature and insistence upon self government in industry are few salient features of Laski's ideal state which would above all things guarantee a comprehensive system of rights, socialistic property and democratise economic and political institutions. In this sense, Pluralism, thus, as Plato's ideal state, is an ideal for all times. Monoism and pluralism are 'points of view', or 'modes of attack' and not theories.

Political pluralism, negatively defined, 'denies that there is any rigid necessity about the demand for a unified legal and political system'. It asserts that "an amount of loose-endedness is possible and under some circumstances inevitable and even desirable".

Till a class-less, completely pluralistic society come into existence, we agree with Sabine and later views of Laski that every state must face the problem of orderly administration, and whatever kind or degree of monoism that implies will have to be accepted unless one is prepared to go the length of saying that orderly administration is impossible.

Where Coker, Sabine and other critics seem to be mistaken is the assumption that pluralists want to set up a sovereignty-less state, almost all of a sudden. If the aim of other pluralists is this then Sabine and Coker are justified in exposing the basic flaw in their theory. But, as has been explained above, Laski's pluralistic society is an ideal which can be attained only when the conditions like mass education, decent standard of living for the whole people, guarantee of a comprehensive system of rights, decentralization of economic and political authority, participation of workers in the government of industry etc. as detailed in the text of 'Grammar' are fully realized. When all these conditions are achieved the resultant society will be a pluralistic society and a classless society from which sovereignty as coercive authority would have withered away. Sabine prefers to steer a middle course between monism and pluralism. He finds good in both. But unfortunately Sabine does not touch the question whether monism, as absolute sovereignty of the state, will be essential even in a classless society. After all the present class-relations cannot continue for all times. Because we agree with Laski that consent should be the basis of law and political, social and economic relation should be increasingly based on agreement between the citizens and their associations and groups, we are convinced that pluralism is both desirable and inevitable. On the other hand monism is transitional and with the progress in science and sociology it must fade away. It is admitted that in the periods of international tension and cold war monism will flourish, while world peace and material progress will provide nourishment to the plant of pluralism. Although Laski had abandoned pluralism for Marxism we believe that he need not have done so because the ultimate aim of Marxism is classless society which, in fact, is, akin to a pluralistic society outlined in detail by Laski in his Grammar of Politics. It is not possible for all men to realise their best selves in a class state. Only in a classless society can be realized both the economic and political rights which are regarded by Laski as essential conditions of life. Hence we conclude that Laski's pluralist society is a classless society which can be realised when the state or the state sovereignty as a coercive power has withered away.

Recently Sinha in his book "Towards Pluralist Society" has suggested a Parliament of these Houses to overcome the dominance of politics over economics and education. He has broadly divided the functions of the state into three categories: (1) Political, i.e., Foregin Affairs, Defence, Police and Justice. (2) Economic, i.e., Trade, Commerce, Finance, Production, Distribution, etc. (3) Cultural, i.e., education, science, culture and health. According to Sinha, there should be thus "three pillars" on which social and state structure should rest. All these three Houses as 'little Parliaments' will constitute the Parliament, which will decide the major policy matter.

This suggestion appears to have been made from the hint provided by Sydney and Beatrice, Webb when they suggested two Parliaments, Economic and Political.

To the Greek "State was the supreme social institution; they recognized other forms of association as essential, but regarded the position of the state as unique.

The State is in Aristotle's words "the highest of all associations ....Which embraces all the rest".

The main defect in the pluralist theory of which Laski was the most prolific exponent was its "failure to make clear which of the specific functions assigned to the state by the monists they would deny to it". Another shortcoming that to Prof. Coker struck was Pluralists assumption that if only an individual or group be released from state control, then we shall have a condition in which spontaneous action, self-expression and initiative will enjoy free play". This criticism holds ground because Laski himself later realized the defects in a theory that reduced the state to the status of a trade union and yet allowed it to perform 'over-whelming' functions of coordination of the activities of the other associations and of preserving law and order by sitting over judgment in the cases of conflicts between citizens and associations inter-se and between citizens and associations. Laski thus abandoned this anarchy of association for Marxism and allowed the state more powers than what even the legal theorists of monism ever imagined. The pluralist concept of state, perhaps, can be realized only in class-less state of which Marx spoke, or in a Utopia outlined by Plato. So long as coercive power is required to enforce law and justice either of the capitalist or of the communist brand, the state sovereignty will remain a fact whether the pluralists recognize it or not. Laski's criticism of idealists who failed to distinguish state from society and government from state is praiseworthy. We agree with Laski that allegiance of man to the state is secondary to his allegiance to what he may conceive his duty to society as a whole. Like Aristotle Laski defines the purpose of state as promotion of good life. Here he tempers Aristotle with Mill by adding that individual alone is Judge of what is good for him. In this blending of Aristotle with Mill we find Laski trying to move mountains by reconciling authority with liberty.

In search of that reconciliation he spent his whole life. The first stage in his efforts was pluralism and the final stage was Marxism. He started with his two sided attack on the sovereignty of state. At first snatched the sovereignty from the sole ownership of the state and divided it between various associations. But by accepting Marxism he not only returned all the sovereignty that he had first snatched but endowed it with what are commonly known dictatorial powers.

Laski's earlier attack on the sovereignty of the state rests on a blurring of the distinction between sovereignty as a legal and as a political concept. If the target of his critical firing was only legal sovereignty no one would grudge. But when Laski wants us to 'surrender' the whole concept of sovereignty he appears to be confused and mistaken.

This confusion leads to a confusion worst confounded when he argues that the Austinian theory of absolute sovereignty is "enough even in its abstract presentation" and as such "would breed simple servility were it capable of practical application". Austin's concept is legal and non-moral. Laski, perhaps, because of intellectual immaturity, for he was only 23 when he wrote this book based his criticism on wrong assumptions.

Yet, Laski's ability to distinguish state from society is commendable.

The age of *laissiz-faire* has, on every plane of living, drawn to its close. Either we go forward to socialism or we must go back to a industrial feudalism in which the maintenance of a privileged aristocracy of predatory capitalists involves the destruction alike of freedom and democracy.

Thus "a world economy means a world government and we cannot achieve a world government so long as the operating unit of political administration is the sovereign national state". It follows, "so long as we build a world order on sovereignty, when the facts about us have made that principle a clear, our world order, as a going political concern, is a pretty thin and unsubstantial thing, a veil which will be torn aside when the member states in that world order confront their first crisis of serious magnitude".

The principle that nation state must at all costs preserve its sovereignty, belongs to and maintains an age of economic scarcity in which privilege is concerned to preserve by force, claims which it could not defend by reason".

"We shall not persuade men to go down a third time (3rd World War) into the abyss to resume a way of life (capitalism) that decays before their eyes".

Our aim is therefore, find that common faith which enables us all to cooperate in casting off these restraints. Our history will become an ever more tragic drama until by the discovery of that faith, we become able to persuade the world that we are consciously developing alike our knowledge and our power to affirm, and not to deny, the yearning of the common man for creative fulfillment. It is, moreover, urgent to realize with all the speed we may that in this epoch time is no longer on our side.

From his earlier works like Problems of Sovereignty (1917), Authority in Modern State (1919) and the Foundation of Sovereignty (1921), Laski gave the impression that he stood for a political "system which apparently would recognize the complete autonomy of such associations, with the abandonment by the state of any claim to be the sole representative of the general interests of men". The same attitude Laski maintained and elaborated in his "A Grammar of Politics, (1925) and advocated pluralism till his demise in 1950.

References

1. Kingsley Martin — Harold J Laski
2. Harold J Laski — Grammer of Politics
3. Harold J Laski — Communism
4. Holmes — Laski Letters
5. M C Kenzie — British Political Parties
6. Harold J. Laski — State in Theory and Practice
7. G.H. Sabine — Political Theory
8. F.W. Cocker — Recent Political Thought

4

LASKI BESIDES PLURALISM

Before we conclude our comments on Laski's political philosophy of Pluralism and Pluralist philosophy which is the main aim of this work, we must in brief point out the significance of Laski's views on state sovereignty, right, Equality, Liberty.

Also to an extent, in brief his views on nationalism nationality and political obligations.

State Sovereignty

Let us first of all examine Laski's view on State Sovereignty, which is central to Laski's political philosophy and even otherwise it is the crucial aspect with far reaching consequences for the whole society, for all the citizens and also for international relations.

In India during Mugal Rule there was absolute sovereignty of the king. What Babur to Aurangzeb said or wished, through their subordinate rajas or nawabs or ministry, was law. Nobody, Nawab or common citizen, could dare disobey. Similarly under Maharaja Ranjit Singh, Sikh ruler of Punjab, his empire extending to NWFP, and Kashmir, Ladakh, absolute sovereignty of the state vested in the Maharaja. Whatever the sovereign permitted was law. In Russia before communist revolution, Tsar was absolute monarch. So were Louis XIV and monarchs of many States of Europe and Middle East of Muslim and Arab countries and China and Japan in East Asia with majority of their citizens being Buddhists. All their rulers, virtually till the end of 19th century or even till the Second World War, enjoyed absolute power under absolute monarchy. On the other hand in UK monarch was no longer an absolute sovereign. He shared his power and prerogative with the Parliament. In USA, too, the President, of the US was elected by the people and had to reconcile his views and policies with that of house of representative, particularly the senate which was representative of all. The states with two members each and with power to ratify or annual treaties proposed or signed by U.S. President.

To this doctrine of absolute sovereignty of state or ruler Laski was opposed and throughout his writings in books like "A Grammar of politics" and even the one entitled "Why I am a communist". That is why though Laski was proclaimed communist he was all the time considered hostile by Soviet Government of USSR and Communist Party. Curbs on sovereignty will be illustrated by his views on Rights, Liberty and Equality.

Rights

Harold Laski, who along with Sydney and Beatrice Webb and George Bernard Shaw, as founder member of Fabian Society, was mainly concerned with rights of individuals in the state. These rights included the right of becoming a member of an association of his own choice, i.e., of Trade Union, Social and Cultural organizations like the one whose aim is to uplift the social status of neglected and poverty-ridden citizens. Membership of the cultural organization was for the citizens who were interested in cultural activities like music, drama and other activities of cultural nature. Membership of such associations determines a man's choice of friends and associates, his ambition about the career for which these cultural as well as Trade Union and Social Societies provide opportunities to mix up and know oneself, his interests, and capabilities. In the words of Professor Laski "these give the feeling to a citizen that he has found for himself, a power of self-recognition that is an invaluable factor in the achievement of personal harmony. What without them is a chaotic world, becomes a world ordered by the opportunity to do with others who share experience akin to his own".

Besides the above rights to be a member of an association of ones choice depending on his interest or training, Laski emphasis on the right of a citizen to own property in his own name as private property. The right to own private property implies that the owner has the right to dispose off this property or alienate it through gift or to bequeath. Right to own private property means much for the citizen owner as he can sell it when he is in dire circumstances because of loss of job, robbery at his home, fire or other calamity. Here Laski is opposed to the Communistic view that regards property and it ownership as symbol of inequality. So that there is real equality of all citizens Marxists and communists are for the abolition of property right. But during last 50 years or so even Communists have started accepting the view of Laski that property is reward for ones efforts, hard work and labour. State should recognize that right to own private property by is citizens.

Liberty

Though Liberty is associated with rights, yet Laski has emphasized on political Liberty which is different from what is normally spoken and understood as Liberty. Political liberty means citizens right to participate in the government of their country or the state, as it is referred to in political Science. Laski goes back to Aristotle, the Greek philosopher, along with Plato who were pioneer in Political philosophy and liberty in particular. According to Aristotle a citizen (in contrast to slave of that ancient period) is one who is capable to rule and is willing to be ruled. Similarly Laski takes guidance from Rousseau a political luminary who in his famous 'Social Contract' wrote that citizens have a right in sharing the sovereign authority of the state and also have duty to submit to the laws of the state. This liberty in this sense does not mean license to do what a citizen likes to do without regard to the laws of the state. This concept of right as well as duty of a citizen is known as political liberty; in contrast to simple liberty, political liberty involves uniform rights in the state. The first and the primary one is citizens right to vote without fear as favour, just according to citizens own thinking and conviction. Harold Laski in his book, Liberty in Modern state, emphasizes that besides the parliament and State legislature, local self-governing institutions further help in freedom and political liberty of citizens.

Thus right to vote follows with right of every citizens to stand for elections and if capable get elected, even, in modern terminology to become a Minister. So that there is no chance of anybody becoming dictator like Hitler, there must be periodical elections. Similarly citizens, if there is political liberty, in contrast to communist or Fascist Dictatorship, have right to criticize the government and implementation of laws passed by the state Parliament or legislature. Political liberty is meaningless if people's voice is taken into account or considered sympathetically only during the election time. Laski truly has said that more widespread the distribution of authority or power of the state, it is more likely the citizens will be zealous to participate or and enjoy political liberty.

Equality

Equality, too, has different aspects like political equality, economic equality. Spread of these two aspects of equality are essential and it is the duty of the state and its law-making body to find ways and means to ensurc political and economic equality of all citizens without discrimination on account of religion and castes, or where as in India, and many other countries there are a number of religions and sects. In a country where there are fewer rich and many poor, where there are fewer educated and many uneducated, thus, Laski points out "we find always masters and servants" In a society where there are 'rich and beggars' there can not be equality. A beggar cannot even exercise right to vote or get elected or criticize the government. Thus it is for the state to reduce inequalities in education and wealth, if the inequalities cannot be ended overnight. Widespread influence of money, particularly during election times, makes mockery of equality between rich and poor, between educated and uneducated. In this concept of equality, which Laski followed to a great extent, Rousseau's The Social Contract has mercilessly stated "Allow neither rich men nor beggars. These two estates, which are naturally inseparable, are equally fatal to the common good."

Equality before law or for attaining justice in the court is essential if the equality is to be of any meaning. But as RH Towny in his book 'Equality' says "Equality in justice is primary condition for attaining civil freedom the inability of a poor person to employ a counsel, still more to employ really skilful counsel is a fatal bar to his attaining justice."

Equality and Inequality

In his 'The Affluent Society' John Kenneth Galbrith, representing Capitalist USA where inequality had dwindled during 20th century because of development and increase in capital. Galbrith says with unconcealed pride: "In 1900-1909 decade employed workers as a class received 53% of all income. By the decade of 1930-39 it had increased to 67%.....in 1955 the 10th with the highest income received 27% of the total which is to say their income averaged 27 times as much as the lowest tenth........". The affluence in USA saved it from the danger of communism or a revolution.

Though absolute equality is hypothetical still more equality and decreased inequality in any country, not only the USA, saves the country and its people from revolution or political disturbance. That is what Laski and prior to him Rousseau emphasized.

The essence of democracy is equality or determined efforts by the state to attain more equality, particularly in income for its citizens. Thus in a country if democracy is to survive there should be more and more equality of income for all its citizens. The gap between income of rich, super rich and poor and deprived down-trodden should get reduced. Every one cannot have equal power or status in politics or government or in Parliament just as every one cannot have equal aptitude for study of medicine, engineering, technology, law etc. But opportunity rather equal opportunity should be provided to all to pursue the subject of their interest that can be done if the state provides universal education for one and all in similar schools and colleges not that same schools and colleges are meant for the rich who can pay much and poor should go to ordinary government schools and colleges.

Equality of opportunity as outlined above and propagated by Marxists and Socialists like Laski and democrats all over the world is, therefore, essential for the survival of democracy as well as for creation of more wealth and opportunity.

The Purpose of the State

The purpose of the state in modern times is to create such an atmosphere by passing such laws that there is no injustice to anyone, rich or poor, educated or uneducated, employed or unemployed—that there is harmony of impulses; that there is no compulsion or coercion for law abiding citizens. As Laski has said: 'The activities of a civilized community are too complex and too manifold to be left to the blind regulation of impulse; and even each man could be called upon to act consistently in terms of intelligence there would be need for customary standard by which the society in its organized form agreed to differentiate right and wrong. Laski further illustrates: The state, as it was and is, has found the roots of allegiance in all the complex facts of human nature. This nature is a mixture of impulses and reason. The satisfaction of man's primary wants - hunger, drink, sex, clothing and shelter involve associated life and associated life implies the necessity of government.'

Thus the state, the society in organized form, keeps coercive power with itself in the form of police and ultimately army to maintain law and order, to curb agitation if it spread too far endangering the peace and the life of peaceful law abiding citizens. The state has also to keep army to fight external aggression. So long as the United Nations is ineffective in wars between various states and is unable or unwilling to resolve conflicts particularly between neighbors, the state is bound to maintain army, navy and air force according to its need and also capability. In civilized states police is used very sparingly and army to help the police virtually not at all. Coercive force as last resort is essential so as to serve the purpose for which the state exists—purpose being to establish peaceful conditions so that there is progress towards equality of opportunity to attain what one aspires for and has aptitude for.

Nationalism

There have been instances even during 20th century when there was a state without nationality or nationalism. In this respect it is important to say that nationality and nationalism are spiritual or sentimental while state is a political entity. Before 1914-18 there was one state called Austro-Hungary but there was no Austro-Hungary nationality or nationalism. They were two different people aspiring for their separate nation or nationality. In Laski's words resultant nationality or nationhood is because sense of unity. Laski elucidates: "This unity is the outcome of a common history, of victories won and traditions created by a corporate effort. There goes a sense of kinship, which binds men into oneness. They recognize their likeness and emphasize their difference from other men. Their social heritage becomes distinctly their own as a man tends to lend his own particular character to his house. So England only could have produced a Shakespeare and Dickens; so we admit there are qualities in Voltaire and Kant from which they typify the nationalism of France and Germany." Gilchrist further clarifies; 'Nation is a state plus something else; the state looked at from a certain point of view viz that of the unity of the people organized in one state.' Events since 1939 have led to dismemberment of many imperial colonies of England, France, Spain, Portugal and finally of Eastern Europe, e.g., India, Pakistan, Sri Lanka, Burma, Vietnam, Indonesia and now East Timor. Algeria, Morocco, Egypt and much of African, west Asian and Latin American Countries and with break-up of USSR, besides countries in Eastern Europe there are Ukraine and Muslim majority countries which were originally part of czarist empire and became part of USSR.

PART–II : POEMS ON REVERENCE LOVE AND SORROW

1

Mother's Love — Supreme Love

Oh Mother Dear; Forgive me
That I had somewhat forgotten thee
While at a far off station,
Though with my wife and children—
The depth of mother's love, the strength of mother's love.
My life - giver mother
Is almost hundred years old
With one arm broken and hanging
Like a broken branch of tree as old
With one eye without sight
And the other with fading light
Like that of a candle in stormy night.
Last time when I went to pay reverence
At first mother mine did not recognize
When I touched her feet and said:
Mother dear I am your son
I am your "Chan"
At once she opended her eyes
Even in the dimness of her sight
She recognized me
And kissed me
As if I was her son of years five
And not an old man of seventy five

She kept on kissing my bearded face
My arms and my hands
While I kept on pressing her feet.
Mother went on whispering
May my son live long !
May my "Chan" live long
Long live my children
Long live my sons life companion.
At first my eyes were moist with reverence
Soon there was stream of tears of joy and reverence
Mother was kissing me and blessing
And God's name she was reciting
For a long time her feet I kept on touching and pressing
And mother dear continued to shower divine blessings.

2

My Father — My God

Since my youth I stopped believing in God
A creator of entire universe
And life in all forms in sea and land
For me, my father was the only god
He was a saint-soldier, a god personified
Every morning he would recite his prayer
In his work and conduct he was always fair
He would consider everyone honest like himself.
He would not grudge those who harmed his self
That is the reason for grace and glow on his face
As if it was really gods face
Because he was sweet tempered who harmed no one
Instead he helped to the extent possible a needy one.
Oh dear father, my god!
Bless me that I follow your path
I know I cannot be like you
But can honestly try to follow you.

3

Guru Nanak — The True Apostle

If you need a Guru to guide you through
He should be like Nanak Guru
Who used to mind buffaloes in childhood
Worked as honest retailer during his boyhood
Thereafter he walked thousands of miles
With Bala and Mardana on both sides
To preach one-ness of God
He walked upto Kashi, Tibet and Mecca
When Babar invaded Hindustan,
Killing and torturing all who did not embrace Islam
Even saints like Baba Nanak were not spared
Guru Nanak too was imprisoned
He complained to God
The protecter of all
Why the almighty allowed Babar to torture all
Put children and their mother to sword
Who dishonoured and enslaved thousands of women
Sent many to Gazni for auction
Though Baba despised Babar
For acting as Barbarian

He considered Hindus and Muslims alike
Those who did good deeds were divine
Thus Guru Nanak was worshiped by all as a saint
As he had seen the light divine
He would not say 'I am God'
Or son of God
He would not say his word is word of God
Instead Nanak called himself servant of God—
Nanak Das or Nanak Gharib
Not living in palace like temple
Not wearing silk clothes that sparkle
To such a Guru 'Chan' bows with humility
Applies on his forehead sacred dust of his feet
So as to try to lead life of piety

4

Guru Nanak Visits India Again

After five centuries in heaven

Guru Nanak expressed his wish to visit Hindustan

He woke up Mardana who had been with him on earth and in heaven

Almighty allowed him short visit to India and Pakistan

Guruji decided to visit his birth place in Talwandi now in Pakistan

He was surprised to find only Muslims some Sufis and Momin

No Hindus, no Sadhus, no Sikhs to be seen anywhere

Guruji decided to meet Muslim Hajis and Sufis

Then Baba Nanak addressed a gathering of Muslims:

All my life I had preached love and fraternity between Hindus and Muslims

What has happened to all that?

I had walked to Kashi, Puri, Baghdad and Mecca for that.

Muslims told him with regret

Baba Nanak your love for humanity we cannot forget

Our folly and British mischief led to partition of Hindustan

In which lakhs lost their lives in India and Pakistan

From Punjab Hindus and Sikhs migrated to India and Muslims to Pakistan

With tears in their eyes Baba Nanak and Mardana left

To see the impact of his teachings in Hindustan

In Amritsar they first visited Darbar Sahib

Listened to celestial Kirtan from Guru Granth Sahib

Guru Nanak wanted to know whether

They were following his teaching and humility

Forgiveness, honest labour and chastity?

Were they considering all men equal,

All castes equal

Thereafter to see for themselves Baba Nanak and Mardana went round the city

Whether people were hard working and giving part of their income in charity

But Baba Nanak was disappointed to find rich enjoying as never before

And poor suffering, without proper food, shelter and clothes,

Baba Nanak got disappointed and ascended to heaven, complained to God

As he had done during Babar's invision of Hindustan.

That many on earth are cruel, corrupt and communist not believing in God

Countries on earth have become more selfish and ruthless

They kill millions of other countries by weapons and nuclear bombs.

They have no use of God.

Or simply recite name of God

5

Glimpses of Paradise

Decades back I was traveling in train
When I was young, religious without refrain.
Train was moving clank clank
I felt I was being rocked in a plank.
Soon I was asleep
I was dreaming in sleep
But it was as vivid as real:
Guru Gobind Singh's darbar was regal
I stood for a while outside
Listening to celestial music inside
Soon the great guru called me inside
To be by his side
I touched guruji's feet with devotion
I felt I was in heaven
I remained in ecstatic state for ages
Then I realized that I was at guruji's feet
Taking his blessings and feeling great
I felt I had attained enlightenment.
Then someone shook me, I opened my eyes
I realized that it-was-a-dream.
As I was quit educated and modern.

I kept the fact about my glimpse
Of paradise in my mind
Made no mention to anyone of any kind
Unlike real and many fake saints
I continued to lead normal life
Only after four decades of marriage
I told my wife
Before, I could, whatever I felt, write

6
Annoyance

Oh beloved mine
Mother of children mine
If you get annoyed
Everything gets annoyed
My home and office
My gardens flowering bushes
My children and friends
In fact world seems annoyed
Nobody is eating as if it's day of fasting
Nobody is singing, as if it is day of mourning
Nobody is laughing as if its day for crying
Nobody is sleeping as if sleep has taken wings
My beloved! If I also get angry and retaliate
The whole world begins to spin
It would seem heavens would fall
Swallow both of us and all
So I try to please you
And apologise to you
With you annoyed somehow the day gets on.
But when the night falls.
The world stops

There is no rest or sleep
Sometimes we cry or silently weep
And it is midnight.
Then I take up courage to make love to you
Remembering the first might when I made love to you
Then and then we get together
Forget our annoyance altogether
Sleep as two bodies and one soul
But after a week or so you get annoyed again.
It is life's game
To please the annoyed beloved again and again
Just as after winter
One enjoys fragrance of flower and sunshine, during spring times.
So is love more enjoyable after annoyance
More pleasure giving after repentance
This is the cycle of life
For plants and for seasons
For husband and wife.

7

Take up Pen Again

Let me take up my pen
Though I am sixty and ten
I have lost many battles of life
Right from youth I had the life of strife
Fighting against injustice in all walks of life
Many a time I lost hope
With situations that I could not cope
Ultimately I decided to write
Story of my life in poetry and prose
When I look back I find
I had some success to celebrate
And feel I have last small battles
Despite others treachery and deceit
I have not lost the war
Oh 'chan'
Take up the pen once again.
As you have fought and not accepted defeat
So that other should not lose heart
Even after defeat
If they show courage they will win
And success will touch their feet

8

What am I

I am just an ordinary man
Neither well known
Nor completely unknown.
Neither I have reached pinnacle of fame
Nor I have earned a bad name
I am one amongst millions
Neither leader of masses
Nor a blind follower of asses.
I believe in finding my way myself
Not to fallow beaten track
That is why I, many times, fall flat
But I do get up and with efforts walk.
Not scared by friends taunt
That I have not attained what I ought.
I tell them, strife is life
Success is a mix of ingredients five
Honesty, hardwork, sincere, luck and sacrifice
If one of the elements is in short supply
You are unable to take off and fly
That is what I did

When at the age of fifty five
I put a full stop to my own ambitions
Strived to help my children to fulfill their missions
After 15 years I feel happy and satisfied
That my children have attained what I aspired
In their success I feel my victory
That is my life and not just history.

9

Poet and Poetry

I write what I feel with intensity
I am not a poet and know not what is poetry
I tried to follow the path of truth
As I grew I noticed there was lot of falsehood
I lost many years of youth in search of honesty and truth
As I was as ordinary man.
Neither God nor demon
I sometimes faltered
But soon fallowed the path
That I had chartered
As I did not become a go-getter
I remained a mediocre
During my 30 years of government service
Those who were too clever
Got an edge over
But I did not abandon hope
I continued to find some scope
In art, in literature and business
First I tried my hand in journalism
As my articles regularly got printed
I thought I could be a new Marx

Thereafter I drew some sketches and paintings
I thought myself a Picasso in making
I wrote some poems in Punjabi
Then started business to make money
But because of misfortune lost all the money
I continued to be a Government Servant
For thirty years I worked hard
Rose in status and earned respect
So I have no regret.
In due course I did realise
I am an ordinary man and not exceptionally wise
Neither a genius nor a great man
Like most of you I am just a family man
Whatever I have written belongs to you
As it is result of common experience of all of you
My writings are my experiences and dreams
These are not poems
I am neither a poet nor a preacher
I am just like you a commoner

10

Love Though Eyes

You looked at me from a distance
In our love it was first instance
With those very eyes
That had won me at first sight
Full of love
Outflowing towards love
It created an urge to meet you
To talk to you, to walk with you
But alas! You went ahead
My desire got crushed
Yet there was satisfaction
That I saw you at a function
Though we had not met
Our eyes atleast had met
For love's transmission.

11

Begging For Love

Today I am begging for your love
Because I love you so much
And you love me as much
If today you don't accept my love
You would regret all your life
That I betrayed the one
Who had only loved one
Without lust
With full trust
Who would be mine for ever
And shall betray me never

12

A Question Mark

If you can't say yes, I love you
You also can't say no I don't love you
How can you say no
When you love me so
You neither say yes nor no
Is it that you don't trust my love any more
Or there are restriction from home
That prevent you from expressing your love to me
Which of these is true?
Can you tell me, my love true?

13

Feelings of Beloved from Beloved

We both fell in love at first sight
And thought of each other day and night.
For more than a year
We just talked about our future
How and when we will be together
For entire life and thereafter
Our was pure and unadulterated love
There was not an iota of lust in our love
We never kissed each other
We never even touched each other
When you got convinced of our mutual love
You took determined step to express true love.
Without telling me you knocked at my house
You were seated in our drawing room
Our love was in full bloom
You beseeched me to give my hand
I responded and extended my hand
That too in the presence of my mother and sister
We thought our love has been accepted no matter.
A year passed
My love was lost.
When last time you came to meet me
You were not allowed even to see me

You were asked to go and forget me
And you left without even seeings me
For fifty years we have not met
But memories of true love we have kept
Now I feel how I disappointed you
Of course I never betrayed you.
As my parents were not in favour of our love
For reasons know to God above
I could not have courage to disobey my father
Instead of revolting I decided to suffer
I wept and cried in isolation
Thinking how much you suffered for my inaction.
But you my dearest love !
Did not let me down
By accepting my family's decision
You gave me respect and freedom
I know your love was true
I remember you were sincere and true
You sacrificed your love
For the sake of our true love
Which means suffering in silence
And remembering each other is silence
I too, remember you and love you.
It is true and too true.
Because you have allowed me to live with respect
You have let our love pass the immortality test

14

Unforgettable Love

Why did you look at me with love at first sight?
With that love that has got divine light
Your first look had shaken my heart
And when you broke that love, it broke my heart.
I guess you could not disobey your family
If so why did you meet me almost daily
To express sincere love
To transmit boundless love
But I loved you sincerely and truly
So I cannot forget you mentally
We have passed almost entire life
Suffering silently
But we cannot forget silent romance
That is life's sustainance

15

Love and Life

When I was just of eighteen years
I was raw and pure —
Like spring water of Kashmir
Then you entered my life
When my heart did not know how the beat
And could not imagine love's warmth and heat
When there was only hope
Defeat and despair had no scope
All hopes and ambitions.
You promised to be my life companion.
Were coated with optimism
Then you entered my life.
Smiling through your eyes
You shook my body and soul
You had ignited in me love and hope
But alas!
After all that there was loss
I lost you
Still I thank you
You short lived association.
Taught me how to face life's tough examination

16

Oh God Help Me

Oh God! Why are you playing with me
Why have you chosen to torture me.
When after crying
I sit down for pondering
You bring back my beloved
To test me and my love for my beloved.
Oh God! I pray!
Don't keep me from my love away
If you are convinced of my sincerity
Then give my beloved to me for eternity
But please God! Remember —
She is mine for ever
If it takes long for me to come to your expectations
Don't be in a hurry to fail me in love's examination
Promise that you would not give her to anyone
And give my beloved to me and to no one

17

To have a Servant or Maid

There have been many instances
Where trusted servants have committed crimes
They have even murdered their master
They have not even spared whom they called father
And treated lady as their mother
Their children as their brother or sister
In many instances they betray
For money for gold they crave
With the help of a criminal whom they know
To share the booty and escape to neighboring land
Some are caught by police
Other evade the police.
But to the dead it makes no difference
Whether their killer is caught or goes free
To the family it is psychological depression
Some wait for years to see the killer hanged
Or for life sentenced
Similar is the story of having a maid servant
Some are greedy and wait
For the opportunity to rob and escape.
For years such evil intention they hide

Who sometimes kidnap children or demand ransom
It is difficult to prevent such crimes
Some old couples cannot do without servant or maids
As their children are abroad
Some of whom have lost even family bond
Because of fast life abroad
It is a moral crime to leave old parents alone
It is a sin if nothing more.
Old people should live with the children
Or grown up grand children
Or in joint family which is real home
Or state sponsored old peoples home
But come what may be never alone
Lonely flat or a mansion cannot be home.

18

Beauty and the Beholder

What is beauty?
It does lie in the eye of beholder
But there is pure and sure beauty —
Which everybody adores
Whether in sculptor
Or in architecture,
In mountains and streams
In sea streams and beaches
In men of good health and nature
In woman of good looks and feature.
Still all cannot appreciate
Because one who have time, knowledge, culture
Can alone appreciate.
As to why Taj Mahal was built by Shahjahan
Just to disclose his love for Mumtaz
When thousands of labourers had to work
With meager wages but no reward.
Similarly beauty in women is appreciated
Mostly by rich and well-to-do
Other have no time to care
They even criticize beauty contest

Of most beautiful women to be at their best
Others love simple village beauty
Without wake up and sparkling dresses
Yet beauty is nature's gift
Which only man can appreciate
Create in stones and paintings
To imitate nature
To appreciate nature

19

Dedication

Dedication is coined in heaven
As in it all the goodness is laden
One can be dedicated
By heart and soul
First and foremost is dedication to parents
If one is dedicated to his mother and father
He can be dedicated to wife or husband
If one is a dedicated son or daughter
Then he would be, in time dedicated father and mother
A dedicated brother or sister
A dedicated friend
A dedicated wife or husband.
As dedicated soldier who lays down his life
Without thinking of children and wife
As a dedicated officer or worker
He cannot be a shirker
He cannot think of taking bribe.
One who is dedicated
His priority is not self
But in whatever situation he is to help
At his own cost
One who is dedicated in thoughts words and deed
He is apostle of goodness and good deeds

20

Thoughts and Deeds

Above all what matters in man is his thoughts
If one is clean in his thoughts
He is nearest to God
He is at the feet of his lord
He cannot do wrong
He cannot advise others to do any wrong
He cannot be selfish
He cannot talk rubbish
His will be bright
As if there is light
Others will take inspiration from him
Even some may worship him
Many will just praise him
Many more will fellow him
Because of his noble thoughts
He is not greedy, neither can be bought
Just as his thoughts and deeds
Are like pure seeds
Which sprout and germinate
More good deeds —
To harm no one

To help the needy one
To care for the down trodden
Not to consider it a barter
Not to have ego
Noble thought and good deeds
Make a man healthy and wise
He may not have worldly wealth
But he is blessed with nature's gift
More he spends more it increases
As no thief or robber can steal it.

21

On Reading and Writing

If you are literate
Good habits you want to cultivate
Then go on reading
Books of all types without ceasing
You should keep on reading and writing that you like
You diary, poems, fiction or what you like
With truth and sinerety without fear or favour and with absolute clarity
Whether what you write is appreciated or not
Whether what you have written is published or not
You should be satisfied with reading and writing
And should continue reading and writing
As long as your heart is beating
As long as you are breathing
That will keep you busy
That will keep you happy

22

Master and Servant

Since times immemorial landlord master has been lord
And servant treated as menial sometimes worse than a dog
There has been sea change during last century
Slaves became masters and free citizens of their country
But in poor countries servants continued to be like slaves
Rich became lazy, easy going and believing in show
Their status in society depended on number of servants
Number of cars, chaufers and darbans
Middle class too engaged small boys and poor girls for domestic work
They were paid poorly and given left out and stale food
Not allowed to go out and play and roam
They are denied education and their own pleasure.
Masters enjoy the life of luxury
Their children enjoy all the freedoms without misery
The contrast is so apparent
Poor child is in hell and the rich in heaven
One cries out his heart
And the other enjoys his life and cares not.

23

Compromise

Some say if one is right
Come what may one should fight
Not bend even a little
Not hesitate to fight to finish,
On the other hand some say life is a compromise
Without compromise it is constant strife
Which can cause worries to one and all
Which can lead to steep fall,
What should one do to lead normal life?
Whether one should abandon all fight
And lead life of a coward always in flight
Ready to compromise even if one is cent percent right.
Life is not smooth sailing
One has differences with many and with some hostility
Even a child tells lies to avoid scolding or beating
He has to be corrected so that there is compromise no beating
As a young man one has more problems
As one has aim in life
He has to face many obstacles to succeed in life
Most of the difficulties require compromise, a few strife
As a married man has to compromise with wife

Because wife is demanding time and security in life
One has to compromise for the sake of children
As their love and future is highest concern.
As you grow infirm and old
All that glitters is no longer gold
You depend on children more often
You have to listen to their harsh remarks quite often
You keep quiet so that children prosper and attain height
And your children are ever happy and bright.
Happiness from childhood to old age requires compromise
Otherwise life is meaningless and not worth the strife

24

Lunatic

Lunatic is one in assylum with torn clothes
Or abusing all the time friends and foes
Or walking aimlessly in streets and roads
Unknowingly throwing stones on others
Or laughing for hours or crying
Sometimes consoling other by playing the role of doctor.
Hardly one out of thousand is lunatic by birth,
Because of genetic defect.
Others become mad because of neglect by society
Either because of heavy loss in business or extreme poverty
Some have lost balance because of betrayal
By either wife or beloved or for landing in jail
Some who consider themselves god
Go on giving sermons even if prevented to speak
Lunacy is a psychological problem with most
If poverty or loss in business or loss of a dear one makes one mad
Then half the population of a poor country would be mad
If one has will power one cannot become a lunatic
He will fight for justice and set an example for would be lunatic.

25

Betrayal

Faith and loyalty seem to have taken wings,
False praises of corrupt and dishonest everyone sings
Many are disloyal to their children's mother
Many to their sisters and brothers
Worst betrayals are of those who betray their mother
Or motherland for money or for settling in other land
Some use money and lust
To gain power and trust
Somc kill their kith and kin.
Some in the name of religion
Kill innocent men, women and children
So many saints came to grapple
But their teaching were of no avail
So long as there is greed and lust
Betrayals will not vanish from earth
Under system of social security in a state it may fall
As there will be no poverty but full employment
Under capitalism without social security betrayals would flourish
Till get-rich-quick greed does not varish.

26

Wine

Every one who takes wine does not become alcoholic
Not all those who drink wine are considered drunkards
Similarly all those who don't touch wine are not saints
They may or may not be taking other intoxicants.
Some drink to forget worry
Others to enjoy and be merry
Some to show that they can afford to drink and enjoy
Others drink to take rest, after the hard work of day
Some drink with friends to strengthen friendship
Others to say hell to friendship.
Some drink to make love
Others drink to forget frustration in love.
Some drink to make love to reluctant wife
On her refusal she gets beaten because she is wife
Those who are cultured and sensible drink to enjoy
Those who are uncultured and rogues drink to destroy.
Wine is like a fire
If it is within control it gives warmth
But if it gets out of control it shows its wrath
It destroys all, wife children home and health.
Wine is like electricity, too

It gives all the modern comfort.
It makes poet of an ordinary man
Brings humility to a noble man
But like electricity if wine over–powers man
It destroys everything including peg and man
It destroys health and faith
It makes life hell and close to death

27

Divorce

In rich and western countries divorce is quite common
For some it is not unusual, for others it is fun
But for poor countries it is more often a tragedy
For the rich in rich countries as well as poor countries it is a comedy
Divorce for Muslims is enshrined under Quranic law
A Muslim can have four wives and divorce one or all under Muslim Law
Without going to court of law.
The wife has no protection under civil law
He has to say before Qazi talaq there times
She ceases to be his wife in no time.
Divorce is now becoming common in countries like India
Because upper classes are immitating west without caring for culture of India
As joint family system is breaking
For good old values of security, love, and respect people are not caring
They just want to enjoy one and then another
Without bothering for future of children and their mother

28

Adoption

In modern times many concepts have changed
Man's ideas and aims are no longer the same
His concept of love has changed
Now for many marriage is no longer a sacred bond
Far so many it is marriage of convenience
Children are no longer gift of God
They can be produced in and outside wedlock
As test tube babies
Or still through newer scientific method
For married woman it is no longer essential to be a mother
Who conceives, gives birth feeds her own child
On one side there are unmarried mothers
On the other there are gays and lesbians who cannot have child
On the one side there are unwanted children
Out of wedlock or through sin who are just abandoned
On the other end there are organisations who arrange adoption
Lucky ones get adopted by rich and educated
Who could not or did not have children of their own
And so adopt the unwanted as their own
They have adoption ceremonies and prayers to God
They consider the adopted child as gift of God

To make there lives happy and purposeful
To make their family absolutely complete and full
In respect of love for the child
There is competition between husband and wife
They love the child as their life
With the innocent talk of the child they smile
The child is blessed one
The couple that adopted the child too, is blessed one.

29

In Coma

The patient, is coma
For relatives it is trauma
Because the patient is old
Doctors just come see and console
Treatment is going on, doctors attending every day tell you
It is quite painful to see daily the patient in ICU
In the same condition day after day
Talk to sisters and doctors but to no avail.
Thus we wait patiently for the day to come
When his life's journey comes to an end
The moment doctors declare him dead
We take urgent steps to donate the eyes of dead
So that two blind can get the sight
Eye bank staff comes at midnight
Examines the dead and go back with his eyes.
We heave a sigh of relief with belief
That we have done a good deed
Though man is dead his eyes will see the light.

30

Guest and Guests

There are guests whom you receive with open arms
Shower on them all the love and courtesies
That, too, to the best of your ability
They, too, respond with love and sincerely
When they want to leave
You request them to stay on and not to leave
Such a welcome guest may be blood relation
Or an old friend and no relation.
Then there are other guests
Who enter your home as ghosts
They get cold treatment
But insist on staying despite cold treatment
Sometimes even they refuse to go
Even if they are requested to do so
Thus they become headache
They show love to children which is false
Ultimately we pray for the day of deliverance
From unwanted guest's presence.

31

Doctor who Cures and Cares

There are doctors with degrees but no knowledge
There are doctors with degrees but no interest in patient
There are doctors who prolong treatment to get more money
There are doctors with fake degrees who are cheats
There are Hakims whose herbal knowledge cures some
There are saints and safis whose pious heart cures some
Then there are doctors who are competent but selfish
They cure only the rich.
Finally there are some doctors who are gods on earth
They are competent and also best at heart
They treat the patient with devotion
There is glow on their faces of satisfaction
Curing and caring the patient is their mission
It is they who are pride of medical profession.
But alas the cream of Indian doctors goes aboard
But by their dedication they make India proud
Medical education converts man into an angel
Unfortunately there are many who become doctors to swindle
As they have paid capitation fee in tens of lakhs
They in particular on becoming doctors who want to earn lakhs
To recover the capitation fee whether the patient lives or dies

32

India's Independence

India won independence in forty seven
Did citizens of India get heaven
No, instead for millions it was hell
Lakhs died during partition riots
Crores lost their homes and hearth
Trains full of deadbodies crossed both sides of Wagha border
As there was anarchy, insecurity and death
For months there was no law and order.
But leaders were jubilant that they had became rulers
They got what they aspired for, for many years
Lesser leaders became rulers of provinces
With banglows, cars they started living like princes
Instead of thousand of British who came to India for loot
Now there were lakhs of Indians who indulged in loot
As a result there is more corruption all round
No leader heeded the advice of honest and old
For majority independences was symbolic
Union jack was lowered and national flag hoisted
Poverty for poor became more widespread
On the other hand rich became richer and feasted
Here and there, there was resentment and revolt

But rich rulers continued to rule by creating favourable vote
bank to vote
Though there were scandals and scams untold
Wealth of India was pocketed by politicians without hold
Though many Indians in science and technology had made mark
In USA and UK they obtained eminence by their hard work
But even intelligent Indians in India failed to get recognition
Because of corruption, nepotism which caused frustration
In twenty first century India is sure to break
Shackles of corruption and economic dependence
Ring of poverty and ignorance too, shall break
And our India shall attain real independence and be great
We have just to work hard, pray and wait

33

Freedom of Man

It has been said 'Man is born free'
But infact only rich men in rich countries are free
The poorest of poor countries are still slaves
They have no work, no food and no shelter on themselves
Some are worse than cavemen
They are just in name human.
The struggle of man to be free
Is as old as when man started walking on two feet
Learnt to light fire by striking two stones
And to kill wild animals for food with sharp stones
Thus struggle to be free from animals came to an end
But immediately domination of strong over weak started
Which led to slavery that got enshrined
It was endorsed by religions as God's command
To suffer silently in this world
To enjoy the fruits is next world.
But quest for justice and equality of man continued
Greek philosopher Socrates was tortured
He was forced to drink cup of poison and thus executed
Many saints who preached freedom
From man's bondage, slavery and serfdom
Were stoned to death, hanged, burnt alive, executed or crucified

Karl Marx became a messiah for equality
For sixty years Marxism was adopted by half the world
Though with the collapse of USSR it got a set back
But its principles got enshrined in many countries of the west
Despite its collapse it showed without getting equity man
won't rest.

34

Alms

One who gives alms he does with smile and grace
One who receives alms he does so with a smile but disgrace
One who gives alms is happy that he has pleased his God
One who receives, heaves a sigh of relief that it is a gift of God.
But why alms are given and received?
It is a comedy and tragedy combined
Tragedy is mostly of poor countries
It has been perpetuated by rich countries
In rich countries for unemployed there are doles
In poor countries for unemployed there is starvation and black holes
In poor countries the rich exploit the poor
Because the state has not cared for the poor
It has not provided universal education for all
It has not enshrined in constitution right to work for all
Nor shelter for all
Nor old age pension for all
If state takes responsibility to provide minimum needs for all
Then there will be no beggars begging for alms

35

Strength in Weakness

You are considered a coward
Because you don't fight to the end to get reward.
When cruelty reaches beyond control
You ponder at the consequences, then hold
You don't fight to finish but withdraw
You change your way so that there is thaw
When matters cross limit
You keep your mouth shut.
Your love was true
But unlike modern day Romeo
You didn't take to violence and
Ending your own or her life
Your accepted defeat in love to lead normal life
Finally you had an educated wife
Thinking it requires courage and sacrifice
To suffer, with broken heart is not cowardice
This proved to be first step
To fight the battle of life.
Where there is victory, after defeats and strife.
One often has to loose small battles
To win the war of life.
Whether it is in love or war

Between two countries
Or it is a would war
To withdraw is wise
So as to organize
To give the enemy surprise
And win the war or battle of life.

36

Good Deeds

If you return evil for evil
Blow for blow
What will be your fate?
You will be worrying all the time —
When the other one will strike?
You will not be able to lead normal life
It is in your interest to be in peace and harmony
Forget and forgive the so called enemy.
He, too, will realise folly of hostility
And clash of ego and its futility
To do good is a spiritual pleasure
What no wine can give in any measure
Nor any deity or continuous recitation of prayers
Nor any holy man or his advice
Because good deeds are holy and without vice

37

In Children One Sees God

It is said all children are creation of God
All are equally dear to God
But in fact there are children of rich parents
And children of poor parents.
Rich children live in luxury and move in cars
While, poor children live in Jhuggis and wear rags.
Rich study in public schools
Poor children seldom or never go to schools
How can all children be equally dear to God?
If at all there is God.
Rich children's God resides in big marble temples
While poor mans God lives in a jhuggi or road side temple
Rich man's God is dressed in costly silk and gems and jewelry.
Poor mans God is poor like him, with the ordinary clothes without canopy
Rich mans God gets choicest fruits and sweets
While Poor mans god gets a few banana and a coconut
Thus there seem to be two gods, not one God —
One for the children of rich moneyed and landlord
Other for the poor uneducated and unemployed
Thus most poor children are not bothered about God
Rich celebrate heavily for their rich and bejeweled God

38

See No Evil

One who can see, will also see
Whatever comes before him, good or evil
If he shuts his eyes from evil
How will he differentiate between good and evil
If he tries to see good in everyone
He will not be a man but an angel
One who does not see evil
How can he fight evil?
If he runs away from evil
He is coward and not an angel
Those who always talk sweetly
May not be sweet really.
They might be sycophants
Who praise others for their own interest.
Those who talk in harsh tones
Are not always cruel
Their harsh tones may be warning against evil
Which is better than soft tones laced with evil.
If one's intentions are good
Harsh words are like honey dew
If intentions are bad
Good words pierce like bullet and arrow.

39

My Accident

I was rushing home on my scooter on a highway
Suddenly I saw a motorcar coming straight in my way
Thereafter I don't know what happened
When consciousness regained
I found myself lying on footpath
With blood dripping from my head
I saw my scooters front wheel and handle away
I demanded water to drink
I felt I was at death's brink
I tried to get up to see if my legs were intact
And my hands and other limbs not broken but intact
There were many persons around me
To seẹ whether I was dead a alive
That is why motor car could not get away
I asked the owner to take me to hospital.
In Safdarjung Hospital I was not attended to,
Saying it was a police case.
I was shocked but helpless
Requested that I should be taken to AIIMS hospital
In the meantime I had became fully conscious
I realized the conflict between medical and police system

So I told the doctor that car driver was not at fault
I would sign papers as you want.
I beseeched the doctor on duty that I should be attended to
at once
Because of bleeding from head I was tense
Soon my wound was stitched, dressed
Car driver became kind.
Gave me helping hand.
On reaching home I realized
How faulty and senseless was our system
But for my presence of mind,
I would have remained on emergency table and died
It was because of blessings of my old mother
My children and my wife,
That I had survived
How many young men die in road accidents?
Because of police and doctor conflicts

40
Someone's Accident

It was midnight
We were returning from a wedding party late night
When at a crossing we saw a crowd
We got down from our car and found
A scooter lying with ignition on
And scooter driver lying besides unknown
We separated the crowd
My young son with the help of one
Put the injured unconscious in our car
We took him to the nearest nursing home.
The doctor on duty examined and proclaimed
Injury on the head is deep
It would cost lot of money
Who would pay the money?
If it is a police case
Who will face?
I promptly said: please doctor revive the patient
Whatever amount it would cost I will pay
If it is a police case I will face
Doctor got my signature at many places
And directed me to arrange necessary finances

I rushed home to get the cash.
Thank God when I returned the unknown patient could talk
I paid doctor's fees with thanks
And got the scooterists address
From his eyes we could read his thanks
Then I told my son to take him to his residence
As his family must be worrying and even crying.
On seeing her husband getting out of car
His wife and children came out near the car
And when my son explained
How he had brought her injured husband
She with tears of joy in her eyes said:
My brother you have saved my husband
My children's father
You have been for us a God.
My son replied: my sister I did
What I should have done
My son returned home saying
I am happy Papa ji at your instance I have done a good deed
After my son went to bed I brooded
How many accident victims die unattended
Because of lack of courage in masses
And fear of police in such cases.

41

Hiring a Cycle

I was lying in a hospital bed
Suffering from a disease that is dreaded
For which so far there is no cure and no remedy
It is death that is telling you to be ready
I know my end is near
But why should I worry and care
I must do whatever I have to do
As fast as I can do.
I was feeling like a small boy
Who doesn't have his own cycle to ride
He hires one from a cycle shop
Goes on cycling tell his time comes to a stop.

42

Your Country My Country

To which country you belong?

Were you born?

First lesson where did you learn?

Which is your mother tongue?

Your ancestors came from Jehlum now Pakistan.

You were born is Quetta in Baluchistan.

But you are neither Baluch nor Pathan

You studied in Patiala after country's partition

But local people did not consider you their own

You were called refugee from Pakistan.

You graduated with honours and get your Masters degree from Allahabad

Finally in search of Job you came to Delhi.

And became a citizen of nation's capital Delhi.

This is a strange world

Old boundaries are getting demolished.

New countries are getting established

In some countries religious freedom is coming to an end

In others fanaticism and terrorism are being fed

With UNO becoming effective and strong

World is moving towards peace and one world
But some countries are getting divided
Million are on the move leaving their homes behind
Many have forgotten their mother tongue and place of birth
They have become citizens of world
Whether it is another province of their own homeland
Or America, Europe or England

43
Temptation

There are many temptations —
Like the one to get rich quick
By befooling someone
By killing someone
By forging cheques and documents
Cheating public and government by fake notes
Selling ones property to so many
And facing life long agony.
Then there is temptation to lie
To get credit for success in life
Get other's research papers published in ones own name
To get name and fame
Even though in frustration the real author commits suicide
But one who steals gets further rise.
There are political temptation to remain in power
Stroking the devastating fire of corruption
One temptation's success leads to another temptation.
But one who shuns temptation is wise,
Secret of good life is strife
Honest living is sublime

Hard work is divine
Such a person rises in his own estimation
He is like divine creation
He is his nation's pride
His children and family's guide
He is model for all
And is praised and loved by all

44

Mistakes

Everyone commits mistakes.
Even God, if there is one has committed mistakes.
By creating dark continent in Africa
And white men in Europe and America.
By giving too much to too few
Allowing suppression of many by few
Allowing indiscriminate killing of all
In earthquake, floods, wars and famines
But man's mistakes too, are many.
He has created caste system to subjugate many
No God or man can forgive crimes for property
If a brother gets killed by his brother for property
If a daughter-in-law is burnt for dowry
Or a daughter sold for money.
Can anyone forget or forgive
Nazi Germany killing six million Jews
By putting them in gas chambers
Or Americans killing millions of Japanese
By dropping atom bombs.
Oh God you are certainly not supreme
Had you been so there would have been no extremes
Fabulous wealth with few and poverty for millions
Exploitation by few of millions

45

Work and Work Culture

It is truly said "work is worship"
But in India many don't work they only worship
Because they have either no work or shirk work
Many consider work as curb on their freedom and worship
They worship many kinds of gods
Some in stones, some worship Holy books or cross of Christ
Modes of worship are also of many kinds
Many worship in temples, churches and mosques
Budhist worship Budhas statue and stupas.
Sikhs worship Holy Granth in Gurdwaras
Some keep fasts while others enjoy feasts
All these customs are to please gods
Whether they ever are seen or not
In India too much time is spent on worship
All this leads to loss of work and even will to work
And worst, a tendency to shirk work
And to go on strike
On grounds of injustice or for pay hikes
In India work is seldom worship.
For many only worship is work
This destroys the work culture

This makes difference in India and Western culture
While in West, America and Japan
People work with dedication and for more productivity
Indian workers are not concerned with productivity
That is the reason for India's poverty
Unless worship culture is replaced by work culture
Or worship culture provides encouragement to work culture
India will remain backward in industry
Though many Indians have excelled in information technology
If "work is worship" is enshrined and propagated
In due course India will score superiority over West

46

Child and Grandchild

To have a grand child is just great,
It is a memorable event to celebrate
You are elated, you are excited —
To see the little one that nature has gifted
Even more than when you had your own child
There is more joy in grand parent loving a grand child
When they had their own child to grow
They could not so much care as now
As young parents they were busy in caring for livelihood
But now they had all the time to enjoy
Grand Child's childhood.
When both husband and wife work
They leave the child in care of a maid
Whose aim is in getting food and paid
Child suffers absence of mother
Her love, smile and laughter
Many working mothers have to regret
For their child's long or short neglect
Some quit the job.
Or change to less time consuming job
But when they grow old

They have no job to hold
Their children are married
Some in India and some abroad
After long wait for the blessed day
On seeing grand child they are full of joy
They shower love, fondle and play
And pray for grand Child's long life night and day
They get purpose to live long
To see the grand child progress and get along
They bless their grand children
Grand parents call their grand daughter
Who has come to please them long after
They also call her "little angel"
For them she is goodness personified as an angel

47

Muslim Rule and Sikh Rule

Punjab is on the route of India's invasion

Muslims used the route for Islamic invasion

After conquering Afghanistan

Which was, for long, part of Hindustan

Where before coming of Islam Hinduism and Buddhism flourished

But, as elsewhere, Muslim invaders, when entered Afghanistan,

They killed all who did not embrae Islam

Destroyed all temple to expand the world of Islam

After conquest of Afghanistan Mughals entered Punjab

Then invasion after invasion continued though Punjab

Ancient seat of Hindu religion and culture was Taxila

Which had been destroyed in the name of Allah

All Hindu and Buddhist temples in Sindh and Punjab were destroyed

Millions of Hindu girls were molested and enslaved

During next five hundred years Punjab was trampled

Punjab was looted

Punjabi women dishonored

Somnath temple in Gujarat was invaded every year

Sacred idols of gold destroyed and taken away
Even the doors of temple went the same way
With the coming Babar Muslim Rule was consolidated
But forcible conversions and killing continued
Then Baba Nanak came to plead
That all men are equal in the eyes of Allah
Those who killed non-Muslims in the name of Allah
Infact displease, annoy and attract wrath of Allah
As only good deeds are expected by Muslims by their own Allaha
But that was to no avail
Nanak and other saints and Sadhus were put in jail
Despite all those sufferings
Nanak along with Muslim disciple Mardana went on preaching
Equality of all men,
Fraternity, peace and harmony between all men
Some mutual understanding developed in Akbar's time
Which was subverted in Aurangzeb's regime
Under whose orders, Guru Tegh Bahadur was executed
As he refused to be converted
His son Guru Gobind Singh vowed to end Muslim cruelty
He organised Khalsa Sikhs to fight against Aurangzeb's
militancy
But Muslim cruelty remained
Guru Ji's two younger sons were bricked alive and executed
Militant Sikhs and Hindus continued to fight
Many times huge Maughal Armies surrendered before their
might

Then history of India remarkably changed
Under the Khalsa Army of Ranjit Singh
Muslims were crushed in Kashmir and Peshawar
Sikhs conquered and ruled Punjab, Kashmir and part of Afghanistan for thirty years
The Afghans of Peshwar after surrender cried
Khalsa–ba–Khuda Bashad—The Khalsa has become God
The Sikhs ruled like Khuda's children
They treated conquered Muslims as brethren
No killing of innocents
No conversions
Not a single Muslim women was molested
Not one Muslim Women was enslaved
So long as Sikhs ruled
In stark camparison to Muslim rule that failed.
Sikhs would have won against British and British Indian Army
Had Dogras not conspired with British and the Army.
As Shah Mohamad a contemporary poet wroter.
Sikhs squeezed the Britisher's blood as one squeezes lemon
But for Ranjit Singh Sikhs last though they had won

48

Hindu and India

Hindus of Hindustan have mostly been peaceful
They believed in and performed religious rituals
Caste system divided them, so they could not face the invaders
Their many languages and cultures differed
Thus they could not give united fight to invaders
Whose aim was to fight and conquer
As Hindustan from Kashmir to Kanniyakumari was
Amalgam of many small linguistic States or nations
Thus invaders could conquer one or two such or nations
And leave many as independent nations
Ashoka the great tried to consolidate
Hindustan into one great Nation
But Kalinga war and the bloodshed
Touched his heart and he was changed
He believed in conquest of hearts
Not of countries and lands
He sent Bhikshas to spread Buddhism
To Lanka, China and South East Asia
To preach Buddhism and spread message of peace
But after his death they embraced Hinduism
Hindustan once again got divided
Into castes, communities and small 'countries'

It tempted aggressive Muslim and West Asian Countries
They went on
Conquering and looting
For many centuries
With sword and fire
Conquering, killing and converting to Islam
Some opposed them
Thus fighting and conquering went on for centuries
Till Akbar had sense to bring peace
Between Hindus and Muslims
Preached Deen Elahi to both Hindus and Muslim
But did not last long
Aurangzeb with aim to convert all Hindus
Millions were converted and millions killed
Guru Tegh Bahadur's martyrdom was a turning point
Guru Gobind Singh inspired Hindus and Sikhs.
Sikh who became militant Sikhs conquered Jammu & Kashmir and Ladakh
Also upto Peshawa which was part of Afghanistan
Hindus and Sikhs under Ranjit Singh
Subdued Muslims and captured North Hindustan
But still Hindustan could not be one nation
It was left to British to create India into one nation
Once again Hindus failed
They accepted partition in haste
They failed to judge British evil design
Before leaving who wanted to divide the Indian nation
So that Hindus and Muslims fight.

49

Cancer

You have been hail and hearty
For years seventy.
You undergo an operation
You have hardly recovered from operation
When a dear one utters 'Cancer'
Papa Ji has cancer
You feel helpless
Become speechless
Like a man who is threatened with a dagger
Or a loaded revolver
You feel there is earthquake
And roof is falling on you
Or your house has caught fire
And flames have engulfed you
Or the ship in which you are sailing
Is sinking along with you
Or you are driving a motorbike
And a truck is coming straight towards you about to kill you.
But after month or two
You try to understand the disease and it's ways

By studying literature night and day
And meeting others everyday.
Learning about its stages and cures
You start feeling, don't care come what may
I must have courage to live the same way.
There are millions who suffer without medical care or treatment
Form many diseases and they are just waiting for death.
You have enjoyed and lived purposeful life
And so should not fear death you should go doing what you
    want to do
Go on writing what you want to
Work and enjoy till last breath
Leave the world happily when cometh death.

50

Neem Tree

About two decades back
I had severe tooth ache
I went to a dentist of fame
He examined teeth, gums and dental frame
I was suffering from sever pain
He prescribed usual pills to end the pain
On the day of reckoning
Operation tooth was beginning
He examined the tooth once more
Took X-ray to be sure
Injected some sedative close to damaged tooth
Thereafter he tried hard to pull out the defected tooth
But he could get only half tooth out
Oh God: I fainted or there was black out
After spending lot of money in vain
I returned home in pain
Took more sedatives to relieve the pain
But the pain was like monsoon rain
It subsided and attacked, again and again
A friend suggested a novel remedy

To take betel leave with tobacco daily
How could I accept his advice?
When I considered tobacco a curse and vice
I replied: tobacco chewing causes mouth cancer
Tobacco smoking leads to long cancer
He kept quiet
I won the point
A few days later I consulted a naturopath
He suggested a cure which who effective in fact
He described before me qualities of Neem Tree
Neem leaves its stem all were almost free
I read some ayurvedic literature on Neem
And started chewing daily leaves and stem of Neem.
My tooth stopped aching.
I planted outside my home Neem sapling.
In couple of years
Neem tree became my dentist
For the last 20 years I never visited a dentist

51

To My Love

If you were not there
I might have been nowhere
I loved you a lot
But last you at last
Far no fault of mine
I consider it an act divine
Because we loved without lust
We did not much grumble at it loss
Instead we learnt
How love rises ambition to new height
How love ennobles
How in love divine light kindles.
Yet had you not come in my life
I would how been half dead and half alive
I would have no courage of face life
Get beatings and defeats in life
Yet keeping head high and strive
In storms of misfortune to remain alive
For all the failure that come in my way
I only felt destination is far away

But for your love I might have been like a Robot
Maybe I would become great
Doing everything to perfection.
Attaining in everything perfection
I might have become rich like Ambani
Or joined civil service or army
Became a general or an ambassador
Or joined politics and become a minister
Like robot I would have become a perfect
Without soul or any own mind
Love taught me sacrifice
And not possession at any price
Love is not selfishness
It is to the brim full of selflessness
Whether it is for loved person
For parents, sisters and brothers
For wife and children.
For country or countrymen.

52

Dogs and Dogs

There are two types of dogs
Those who are born to dogs
Those who are born to men but by their deeds become dogs
Those natural dogs bark but do not bite
Those men who become dogs do not bark but bite
Dogs by birth are by nature loyal
To those who keep them as pets
Keep them, feed them and love them like their children
They in turn protect them,
Never hurt them.
But human dogs are treacherous
They bite even the virtuous
They bite for selfish reasons their friends
They don't spare even their blood relations.
Which of the two categories of dogs are more dangerous?
Which one is more ferocious?
Natural dogs only bite rarely
Either to protect his master
But human dogs plan before they bite
Those who have come to know of their nature

Avoid them and don't be near
They keep themselves away
And save the day
But those simple and unfortunate ones
Who trust then?
Are either mercilessly finished
Or left to perish
Or live as beggars
However some human dogs get beaten
And thrown to natural dog to be eaten

53

Patience

It is said : patience pays
But too much patience is inordinate delay and betrays.
Then how much patience is required?
To successfully complete the work acquired.
If in watering the plants there is too much delay
The plants will wither away.
If excessive irrigation is done
Flowers, fruits and grains will be none
Similarly in men's work and conduct
Patience must be limited to required extent
Neither too much that is lethargy
Nor too little that is being hasty
Farmer's patience is best to emulate
It depends on his experience constant watch and climate
He ploughs his land sows seeds mechanically or by hand
Irrigates when required
Weeds out wild plants not required
As the crop grows,
His hope and happiness glows
But he does not become lethargics

Continues to be watchful and energetic
Even when the crop is ripe
He is vigilant day and night
Takes precautions and pains against unseasonal attack by pests or locust
From fire and theft
Finally he reaps the harvest pays his debts
And brings home the rest.
He and his family dance and enjoy
His labour and watchful patience has given them joy
Oh men of all professions and trades
All occupations and shades
Avoid too much hurry and inordinate delay
And thus avoid evil day

54

Equality of Man

It is enshrined in many constitutions.
All men are, or born, equal
Their rights are equal
Their opportunities shall be equal.
I ponder how can all men be equal when millions are doomed
Starve and die as they do not have right to work
No means of livelihood
No roof on their head
No medical care for them
For old and infirm there is no pension.
Thus man's equality is a force
If all men are to be equal,
Though born unequal,
They should have equal right to education
No destination between rich and poor
When they grow up,
They should have guaranteed job
Minimum decent wage
All should have access to similar health service

Not that rich go to Five Star Hospitals
And poor wait for admission in General Hospitals.
Unless such provisions for equality are enschived
The constitution, to the uplift of poor, remains blind
Democracy is aristocracy
Mention of equality in constitution is hypocrisy.

55

Mind

Some say his mind is clean and clear
Like water of springs in Kashmir
Without an iota of evil
Without sorrow or fear
He is always willing to do good to others
Without expecting any reward or favour
He does always to everyone good
Because his mind is simply good.
He sees no evil
Because his mind is devoid of evil
There are others whose mind is not stable
Like Hamlet he remains in two minds
He does not quarrel with others
He does not resent status of others
There are yet other who mind
Such person debate and discourse as their mind is not clear
They talk too much
Attain too little
They often quarrel with themselves
But ultimately blame themselves

Findly there are evil minds

Who are willing to join conspiracy of any kind

They want Status at any cost

They try all tricks to be wealthy at any cost

Such evil minds are consumed by fire of lust

But man is born free

His mind too, is born free

Mostly it is the society that makes his mind

Of one or the other kind.

56

Service

Which service is best?
That which is done with donations of wealth
On that which is rendered at the cost of one's health
Or that which comes though mind and heart.
Is it enough to serve a Guru or God
Whose abode is a temple and knowth all?
Or to serve a hungry who had no meal
Or a wounded man so that his wounds heal
Or old parents who cannot see or walk
Or ones children whose careers are yet to chalk.
Who need guidance and money
For higher education or floating a business company
Service without greed
Without regard to creed
Without expectation of reward
Is true service of man or God.
Otherwise it is business dealing as any
With self, God, society or country.

57

Man and God

After man's conquest of moon
God is no longer equated with creation of moon
It is no longer Gods creation
Even it is doubted whether universe is His creation
Moon is no longer considered beautiful
That mothers will not call their sons dear Chand or moon
Some Muslim may no longer break his Ramzan fast
On having a glimpse of moon
Devout Hindus will no more take bath on full moon
They will ignore whether it is full or half moon
Today man has conquered moon
Tomorrow he will reach Mars.
In due course if man survives nuclear war
Man will explore and conquer entire universe.
And God will be confined to temples
Mosques Gurudwaras and Churches
His worshipers will no longer be billions.
They will be hundred thousands or millions
When sun of science shines
Fundamentalism will become a surprise

58

What Matters—Money or Man

In modern age it is money that matters
Whether one is rich or poor
Saint or sinner
Worker or beggar
Because no one can live without food
Money alone can buy food even a sadhu begs for food
A billioner may not care for food
But he too, cannot live without food.
This is age of information technology
To succeed in this profession Money is required without apology
But a Bill Gates is required in this profession
Without him all the gadget are useless
Without man money is purposeless. - .,
Thus it is man that matters more
Money is behind and man is before.
Man is the creator
Man is maker
Without man's efforts and enterprise
Money particularly unearned money remains dead.
Man with his ingenuity created money.

He can create something more to replace money.
Credit cards,

Debit cards, Misuse of money creates new type of crimes

Like attack on WTC

Man finds new ways to end crimes

Nothing remains static, man or money. Everything moves with times.

59

Landing on Moon

My rocket was flying towards moon .
I was at my telescope watching moon.
Sometimes moon appeared its usual round
Sometimes, strange objects, on moon are found
Sometimes moon appears lilly white
Sometimes red like French wine
Sometimes it appeared of many hues
Sometimes as if washed in dew
Sometimes kaleidoscopic
Sometimes microscopic.
Then I got excited to see blue and white rocks
I felt I was about to land on moon
I held my breath
My rocket touched moon with a thud
I opened racket's latchet and jumped out
I got hurt and cried
On hearing my cry my beloved woke up
Put my head on her cap
I opened my eyes and got up
This brought me back from moon to earth.

60

Attack on Golden Temple

Oh Indra!
To remain in power,
You quarelled with supreme power
You ordered attack on Golden Temple
The Indian army attacked with rockets and tanks
Besides destroying Akal Takhat
And damaging darbar sahib
Your army defiled nectar filled tank.
Oh Indra!
You were prime minister of whole of India
You were guardian of all religions and culture of India
How could you forget that
How could you be forgiven for that cruel act.
Attack on Golden temple
Shocked all particularly Sikhs all over world
It was like an attack-had Saudi Arabian army.
Attacked holy Muslim shrine of Mecca
Or if Italian troops had been ordered
By Italian government to destroy Church of Rome
Or some Indian prime minister had ordered
Attack on Kashi or holy Mathura temple

You Indra!
Failed to realize the gravity
Of your selfish act of attack on Golden temple
Thousands of Sikhs including women and children
Were killed or wounded.
As the day of attack was martyrdom day Guru Arjun
And Sikhs had come for a holy dip in holy tank.
Oh Indra!
It is sad and unfortunate that you were killed
By Sikhs in revenge
Just as they had killed Dyer the British General
Who had ordered attack in Jallianwala Bagh.
Earlier Aurangzeb had ordered killing of Guru Teg Bahadur
And Sikhs destroyed the Mughal rule.
By taking up arms against Mughal rule
As Guru Gobind Singh's Khalsa
And under Ranjit Singh's army of Khalsa
Oh Indra!
Had you served India honestly
Subdued your hunger for power
And not ordered attack on Golden temple
You would have lived long and for ever

61

Trains to Hell 1984

Some trains were leaving Delhi
But unlike in normal days no train crossed border of Delhi
And no train from outside, reached Delhi
Every train was held up somewhere near Delhi border
Sikh passengers were being dragged out by lumpins
Who removed their turbans
Those who resisted received blows of iron rods
Their hands feet were tied with their turbans
Or their turbans twisted into ropes
One end tied around their necks
And the other end was pulled by ruffians
Some passenger locked themselves in toilets
Saved their lives to tell others the fate their brother met
A few saved themselves by getting under the seat
So that they could save themselves by holding their breath.
There were soldiers going on leave after defending Indian borders
Or returning from home leave to defend our borders
They too, met the same fate
Inspite of their uniforms and protests
There were some rich Sikhs

Who were looted and done to death
For goondas and their leaders all they wanted were Sikhs
They forgot that they were Guru Tegh Bahadurs Sikhs
Who had laid down his life for Hindu faith and Hindustan
Ultimately when a few trains arrived at Delhi Railway Station
There were only dead or wounded Sikhs
The relatives who came to receive them
Cried and some a fainted at the railway station
Yet some decent men of all faiths offered
Them first aid, water and food
Arranged to send them to their homes.

62

Even God did not Listen

Oh God you are considered omnipotent
But where were you, oh omnipotent !
When sons were beaten to death before their mothers
When young girl were molested before the brother and father
When before sisters their brothers were struck with iron rods
And fell unconscious
When newly wed wives' husbands were dragged
And burning tires put in their necks
When before innocent children their parents done to death
When mothers were wailing for their dead children
When father who were old and infirm could not get up and run
To save their children from certain death
Oh God! Where were you?
When in your world, in your Delhi thousand of
Innocent were being massacred
And the murderers were dancing and drinking.
It appears you are non existent
Oh God! If you are really there, appear
If you are not deaf listen
If you are not blind see and cry
But oh God! You did nothing

Neither you punished the criminals
Nor you helped in ending the crime wave
That continued for four days
Some criminals were punished by the sufferers
But this revenge caused more suffering
More and more innocents were killed
Either by terrorists or by police
This tragedy went on for years
Till time healed same wounds
Oh people! Awake
There is no God in heaven
If at all he is there, he is not omnipotent
You have to guard yourself
You are to help the victims yourself.

63

Genocide of Sikhs and Forgiveness

Genocide of Sikhs was allowed after Indra's murder
When thousands of Sikhs were tortured to death.
Atrocities on Sikhs went on for years
But not a single criminal was punished
Though commission after commission investigated
Yet time has come to forgive and forget
As valiant Sikhs do forgive and forget
By recalling: the suffering and torture of Guru Arjun.
Remember how Guru Tegh Bahadur was martyred
On order of Aurangzeb
How cruelly two young sons of Guru Gobind Singh
Were bricked alive.
Yet valiant Sikhs have to forget
Attack on Golden temple and genocide of Sikhs
Just as they have forgotten
Partition riots of 1947
In 47 lakhs of Sikhs perished
In 84 tens of thousand perished
But tragedy is that in 47 Sikhs were victims
Of British conspiracy instigating Muslims
But in 84 they were killed
By their own army in their own land

64

Demolition of Babri Masjid

Since Times Immemorial in Ayudhya there was
A sacred Ram Temple
Worshiped by Hindus as most sacred temple
Babar the invader destroyed this Gods temple
Virtually no temple of Hindus, Buddhists or
Jains was left standing
All the worshipers were left wailing.
From Turkey to Afghanistan
And what is now Pakistan
Terrorist Babar Killed, Tortured and Imprisoned Lakhs
He imprisoned Guru Nanak and other saints
Guru Nanak even complained to God
As to why the Almighty allowed Babar to invade
Our peaceful land
But as Babar had destroyed
Temple after Temple
To commemorate his conquest he built
On the sacred ruins of Ayudhya temple Masjid
And called it Babri Masjid
With the end of Moughal rule
Came the British rule
Hindu devotees claimed Babri Masjid was

Infact their ancient and sacred temple
British withheld the dispute between
Masjid and Temple
But Muslims were not allowed to offer Namaz
So on doors of Masjid — Temple they put lock
Congress Governments to win Hindu votes
Under Rajiv Gandhi in 1986 removed the lock
Allowed Hindus in part of Masjid to install their lord
With BJP Government in Uttar Pradesh
Plan was hatched to destroy Babri Masjid
Congress Government of Narashimarao approved tacitly.
As no steps were taken to forestall or
Halt this unlawful activity
No troops were sent to prevent demolition
Thus BJP and Shiv Sena completed their mission
Without bothering about Muslim reaction
Sooner or Later that was certain.
In Bombay there was Eruption and Explosions
Killing hundreds of Indian citizen mostly Hindus
Injuring thousands of other primarily Hindus
Destroying vast National property
Jeopardising National unity.
I could not suppress my feelings
I could not shut my eyes
I could not plug my ears
I share with you, my countrymen
Of all faiths and religions
What I saw heard and felt
I could have been killed during partition riots
Or during 1984 Anti Sikh riots
But I am alive my countrymen to tell you all.

Annexure

On extracts from book 'When a tree Shook Delhi : The 84 carnage and its aftermath, By Manoj Mitta. H.S. Phoolka.

Sardar HS Phoolka a senior Advocate who has been pursuing the case of 84 anti-Sikh riots before various Commissions and Shri Manoj Mitta a law graduate from Hyderabad who is a senior editor with *Times of India* and has written extensively on 84 Carnage. Their book gets more authenticity because one author is Hindu and the other is Sikh both eminent in their respective fields as intellectuals.

I was impressed by the analysis of 84 carnage, so I rang up Sardar Phoolka whom I had met with my close friend of 60 years since 1947, Shri SJS Chhatwal who retired as High Commissioner of India in Canada and after retirement was made member of UPSC and retired from Union Public Serivice Commission as its Chairman Sardar Phoolka had read my poems particularly got impressed by my 5 poems on anti Sikh riots. Sardar Phoolka readily agreed to allow me to include Annexure's of their book in my forthcoming English translation done by myself of my Punjabi poems. Sardar Phoolka was rather enthusiastic and said Harcharan Ji you can take any amount of extracts from our book. It will give us pleasure and satisfaction.

So, here are those valuable and startling extracts which show that even President of India, who happened to be a Sikh was attacked and the police looked on, did nothing to arrest the rioters who even stoned President's car. Again, it would be startling to note that General Arora—hero of 1971 war against Pakistan and who received surrender from Pakistan's General Niazi who had agreed to hand area 90,000 Pakistani soldiers to Indian Army as

Prisoners of War—had to be escorted and took shelter in the house Shri I.K. Gujral.

Italics and markings wherever these occur are mine.

The omission paved the way, within minutes, for another attack on Zail Singh, this time, right in front of AIIMS. Raising slogans against him and his community, a mob pelted stones at his cavalcade. The President's car itself was hit. But, being bulletproof, its windows and windshield withstood the attack. His bodyguards, however, sustained injuries while trying to shield the President.

The attacks on the President's cavalcade were widely reported in the next morning's newspapers amid stories about Indira Gandhi's assassination. 'Zail's car stoned, panic in Delhi' was a headline in *The Telegraph,* which said: 'The President's motorcade, as it proceeded towards AIIMS from the airport, was heavily brickbatted. Three cars in the motorcade were damaged, though the President, who was in his bulletproof car, was unaffected.'

Jagjit Singh, an activist of the trade union wing of the ruling Congress Party, was among the many Sikhs who felt secure enough to join the milling crowd of mourners around AIIMS. Despite a delay in official confirmation, the news that Mrs. Gandhi had succumbed to her injuries was out by 1.00 pm. That was thanks mainly to the special afternoon editions of newspapers brought out at a time when twenty-four hour private news channels were still unheard of in India.

In his affidavit before the Justice Ranganath Misra Commission, the first judicial inquiry ordered in 1985, Jagjit Singh gave an eyewitness account of the second attack on President Zail Singh. All the stone pelting, he said, was done by a small group which raised slogans such as 'Giani Murdabad' (Down with Zail Singh), 'Sardar gaddar hai' (Sikhs are traitors) and 'Khoon ka badla khoon' (Avenge murder with murder).

Since the police remained mute spectators to such a grave provocation, the slogans against Sikhs caught on and did not subside even after the President's departure from AIIMS by about 5.15 p.m.

Excerpts of testimonies before the Misra and Nanavati Commissions:

Writer Khushwant Singh before the Nanavati Commission

...........That the same evening Mr. MJ Akbar (newspaper editor) came to my house for dinner. I heard some noise outside on the main road and I went out to check. I saw about 20-25 policemen standing on the road and the mob was looting shops belonging to Sikhs at Khan Market. The policemen were not taking action at all. The policemen did not make any attempt to stop them or disperse them.

...That after some time the mob burnt the taxi stand on the main road.

...That around midnight the gurdwara behind my house was attacked.

Writer Patwant Singh before the Nanavati Commission

...That Air Chief Marshall Arjan Singh (Retd.), Lt. Gen. Jagjit Singh Aurora (Retd.), Brig. Sukhjit Singh (Retd.), S. Gurbachan Singh and I called on the President of India in the morning of 1 November 1984. We spent one hour with the President and told him that numerous Sikhs were being killed all over the capital, emphatically spelling out for him the violence overtaking the Sikhs throughout the city. We made clear that he as the President was morally and constitutionally bound to put an end to it. He replied, 'I do not have powers to intervene.'

I was stunned by this astounding remark. I said, 'Mr. President, you mean to tell us that if the nation is going up in flames and people are being butchered in the streets, you have no power to stop the anarchy and bloodshed.' He kept silent....

Former Prime Minister IK Gujaral before the Nanavati Commission

On 31 October, 1984, I came to know about the attack on Mrs. Indira Gandhi at about 11.00 a.m. I then went to All India Institute of Medical Sciences, and returned from there in the afternoon. Late in the evening, I came to know that riots had broken out in the city and elsewhere. Next morning i.e. on 1 November 1984, after reading newspapers, I contacted the President of India on telephone. He advised me to visit some of the affected areas, and also contact the government. I considered it very odd that the President of India had asked me to do such a thing. On 1 November 1984, there was a meeting of Opposition leaders and therefore, I was picked up by Dr. Farooq Abdullah at about 10.00 a.m. On my way, I noticed houses, trucks, etc. burning. After I returned to my house, I received a telephone call from General Aurora, and I was informed that he, along with Mr. Patant Singh, Air Chief Marshal Arjan Singh and others, had met the President of India, and had returned disappointed by his response. I then went to the house of Mr. Patwant Singh and there we decided to go and meet the home minister, Shri Narasimha Rao. I saw various incidents of burning properties while on the way to the home minister's house, and return. I could see that there was no attempt either to get hold of the people or to extinguish the fire. As I was driving the car myself because my driver was absent on that day, I was stopped on the way twice by the crowd carrying lathis, etc., and shouting slogans. Some of them came near my car, and opened the door and enquired whether there was any Sikh inside the car. During my talk with the home minister, I noticed that he did not know many details about what was happening in the city....

General Aurora was contacted by some army men and after being escorted by army men, he came to my house. So General Aurora and Mrs. Aurora stayed in my house.

Minister for Chemicals and Fertilizers and Steel, Ram Vilas Paswan before the Misra Commission

....That we, a group of four, including myself, Karpoori Thakur, Devi Lal and KR Arya, went in a car up to Tilak Nagar to assess the whole situation. On the way, our vehicle was stopped at many places by mobs. They let us go only after ensuring that there was no Sikh with us. We saw that there was smoke everywhere and there were many groups of miscreants standing at many places....

....One sardarji who was lurking somewhere was beaten mercilessly. He sought refuge in my residence..... The mob attacked my house at about 4.00 p.m. My bodyguard Joginder Prasad Singh and private secretary Mahinder Betha were at the gate. They closed the gate. But the mob surrounded the residence from all sides. Joginder Prasad Singh knows many faces in the mob and can appear as a witness if and when required. According to him, the known figures were workers of Congress (I). They were shouting anti-Sikh slogans..... We managed to save our lives by escaping through the servant quarters situated at the rear wall of the house. Then they caught hold of the injured old sardarji who could not run along with us. The mob threw him alive in the burning garage, where he was roasted alive.....

Former Law Minister Ram Jethmalani before the Nanavati Commission

....My friend Ms. Laila Fernandes came to my house that evening, and she narrated some of the terrible incidents that were happening in the city. We decided to call on Shri Narasimha Rao, the hon'ble home minister at that time. We met him. We mentioned the incidents of fire and killings taking place in the city, and requested him to take immediate steps to stop the carnage. I even detailed some of the steps that were urgently required. They included imposition of curfew and induction of the army. We were with Mr. Rao for about half an hour. During this time, I did not see Mr. Rao giving instructions to any officer, or taking any urgent steps of any other kind. 1 found him listless and unenthusiastic. This could well be his ordinary style of behaviour, or it may be that he too was shaken by the events. I can only say that I experienced acute disappointment on this visit....

Former Law Minister Shanti Bhushan before the Nanavati Commission

....That we visited Shakarpur, Pandav Nagar, and several east Delhi's colonies, and rescued many trapped Sikh families, and took them to the nearest gurdwara .... we also saw many dead bodies of Sikhs who had been killed, and some bodies were still burning.

That we also saw some police officials with their name plates on their clothes, but got the impression that they did not appear to be doing anything much to stop the killings.....

....That it is my firm conviction that these incidents could not have happened without some people organising them, arranging for the mob, and distributing kerosene and other inflammable material to them in an organized manner, with the connivance of the state machinery. If the state machinery really wanted to stop those incidents, they had sufficient means to stop them by opening fire at a couple of places on the first day.

Former Finance Minister Madhu Dandavate before the Misra Commission

When the train reached Tughlakabad Station (on the suburbs of Delhi) on 2 November morning, a large number of persons carrying iron rods, axes, crow bars, etc. entered our train. They were searching for Sikh passengers in the train. They declared that no Sikh would be allowed to leave the train alive. At that time, I found that some Sikhs in the adjoining compartments were pulled down by those outsiders carrying weapons. I found two Sikhs killed and thrown on the platform, and then their dead bodies were set on fire on the platform. The police standing on the platform made no efforts to prevent either the killing or burning of the Sikhs.

Director of MacArthur's India Office Poonam Muttreja before the Nanavati Commission

....On 1 November, 1984, by 1.00 a.m. morning, phone calls started informing me about the water poisoning in Delhi's water supply. I also called a friend in Munirka at 2.00 a.m., informing him of this news. My friend, Shekhar Singh, explained to me that it was technically not possible to do so. At 2.30 a.m., I heard the following on a public address system, 'Aap ke pani mein jahar mila dian gaya hain, kripya pani nahin pee jeaey.' I ran into my balcony and caught sight of a jeep that was moving away from the colony towards the road leading to JNU. The jeep was dark blue in colour and looked like a police jeep.